UNIVERSITY OF
WINCHESTER

Martial Rose Library
Tel: 01962 827306

To be returned on or before the day marked above, subject to recall.

FLAWS AND CEILINGS

Price Controls and the Damage They Cause

EDITED BY CHRISTOPHER COYNE AND RACHEL COYNE

Institute of
Economic Affairs

First published in Great Britain in 2015 by
The Institute of Economic Affairs
2 Lord North Street
Westminster
London SW1P 3LB
in association with London Publishing Partnership Ltd
www.londonpublishingpartnership.co.uk

The mission of the Institute of Economic Affairs is to improve understanding of the fundamental institutions of a free society by analysing and expounding the role of markets in solving economic and social problems.

A CIP catalogue record for this book is available from the British Library.

ISBN 978-0-255-36701-1

Many IEA publications are translated into languages other than English or are reprinted. Permission to translate or to reprint should be sought from the Director General at the address above.

Typeset in Kepler by T&T Productions Ltd
www.tandtproductions.com

Printed and bound in Great Britain by Page Bros

CONTENTS

THE AUTHORS

Philip Booth

Philip Booth is Editorial and Programme Director at the Institute of Economic Affairs and (from 1 May 2015) Professor of Finance, Public Policy and Ethics at St. Mary's University, Twickenham. Previously, he worked for the Bank of England as an advisor on financial stability issues and has been Associate Dean of Cass Business School. He has written widely, including a number of books, on investment, finance, social insurance and pensions as well as on the relationship between Catholic social teaching and economics. Philip has a BA in economics from the University of Durham and a PhD from City University.

Ryan Bourne

Ryan Bourne is Head of Public Policy at the IEA and a weekly columnist for *City AM*. He has previously worked both at the Centre for Policy Studies and Frontier Economics and has written widely on a range of economic issues. He has both MA (Cantab) and MPhil qualifications in economics from the University of Cambridge.

Christopher J. Coyne

Christopher J. Coyne is the F. A. Harper Professor of Economics at George Mason University and the Associate Director of the F. A. Hayek Program for Advanced Study in Philosophy, Politics, and Economics at the Mercatus Center.

Rachel L. Coyne

Rachel L. Coyne is a Senior Research Fellow at the F. A. Hayek Program for Advanced Study in Philosophy, Politics, and Economics at the Mercatus Center at George Mason University.

Stephen Davies

Steve Davies is Education Director at the Institute of Economic Affairs in London. He has held this position since 2010. From 1979 until 2009 he was Senior Lecturer in the Department of History and Economic History at Manchester Metropolitan University. While there he taught courses on a range of topics, including world history, the history of crime and the criminal justice system in the UK, and the history of the Devil. He has also been a Visiting Scholar at the Social Philosophy and Policy Center at Bowling Green State University in Bowling Green, Ohio and Program Officer at the Institute for Humane Studies at George Mason University in Virginia.

Robert C. B. Miller

Robert C. B. Miller is a former Senior Research Fellow at the Institute of Economic Affairs. Recent publications include *Linguistics and Economics: Is Entrepreneurship Innate?* (Economic Affairs, October 2014), *What Hayek Would Do* (Adam Smith Institute, 2013), *The Austrians and the Crisis* (Economic Affairs, September 2009).

Colin Robinson

Colin Robinson is Emeritus Professor of Economics at the University of Surrey, Guildford, UK. He worked as a business economist for eleven years, mainly in the oil industry, before being appointed to the first Chair of Economics at the University of Surrey where he founded the Economics Department. His research is principally in energy economics, energy policy and regulatory economics. In 1992 he was the British Institute of Energy Economics Energy Economist of the Year and in 1998 he was presented with the International Association for Energy Economics Award for Outstanding Contributions to the Profession of Energy Economics and to its Literature. From 1992 to 2002 he was Editorial Director of the Institute of Economic Affairs.

Steven Schwartz

Emeritus Professor Steven Schwartz AM was the vice-chancellor of three universities: Brunel University in London, Murdoch University in Perth and Macquarie University in Sydney. He is the Executive Director of the Council for the Humanities, Arts and Social Sciences, a Senior Fellow at the Centre for Independent Studies, and an Honorary Fellow of the University of Melbourne. In 2013, he was Oliver Smithies Fellow at Balliol College, Oxford University.

W. Stanley Siebert

W. Stanley Siebert is Professor of Labour Economics at the Business School, University of Birmingham, where he has worked since 1980. He gained his PhD at the London School of Economics. One of his interests is 'bad law'. Much of his research shows how the simple economic assumptions of self-interested, informed individuals can explain the adverse response of labour markets to government regulation of wages and working conditions.

Christopher Snowdon

Christopher Snowdon is the Director of Lifestyle Economics at the IEA. He is the author of *The Art of Suppression, The Spirit*

Level Delusion and *Velvet Glove; Iron Fist*. He has also authored a number of publications for the IEA including *Sock Puppets*, *Euro Puppets*, *The Proof of the Pudding*, *The Crack Cocaine of Gambling* and *Free Market Solutions in Health*.

Richard Wellings

Dr Richard Wellings is Deputy Editorial Director at the Institute of Economic Affairs and Director of IEA Transport. He was educated at Oxford and the London School of Economics, completing a PhD on transport policy at the latter in 2004. Richard is the author, co-author or editor of several papers, books and reports, including *Towards Better Transport* (Policy Exchange, 2008), *High Speed 2: The Next Government Project Disaster?* (IEA, 2011), *Which Road Ahead – Government or Market?* (IEA, 2012) and *The High-Speed Gravy Train: Special Interests, Transport Policy and Government Spending* (IEA, 2013). He is a senior fellow of the Cobden Centre and the Economic Policy Centre.

FOREWORD

Price controls have a long history and were used particularly widely in post-war Britain and the United States. They have long been studied by economists and, typically, are regarded by economists as one of the worst forms of intervention in markets. Price controls can arbitrarily prevent many welfare-enhancing transactions from taking place when other forms of intervention, such as subsidies, would have less pernicious effects. The problems of price controls can be especially acute because they are typically imposed in property and labour markets and thus affect whether people can work or where they can live: their effect may be to prevent young or low-skilled people from getting jobs or from obtaining a roof over their heads. The regulation of prices can also prevent market participants from finding new ways to solve the very problems that price controls purport to solve. For example, if controls on the price of energy reduce investment in exploration or new sources of energy, in the medium term those controls may lead to higher energy costs. Similarly, limits on fees in higher education – especially if they are combined with regulation of the sector – may lead to reduced innovation so that low-cost alternatives to current models of provision do not develop.

It may be thought that price controls are uncommon in post-1980, so-called deregulated economies. It is true that they may not be as crude as they used to be; and perhaps their effects are not as pernicious. However, price controls are alive and well in several major industries which cover a huge percentage of national output. University fees are limited to £9,000 per annum; railway fares are capped; short-term consumer finance and also pension products are to be subject to a charge cap; there are proposals at different stages in different parts of the UK for the minimum pricing of alcohol; and the UK also has a national minimum wage. The minimum wage is currently set with the aim of minimising its employment effects, but both major parties have indicated a desire to set it according to political considerations. Furthermore, two of the battlegrounds in the general election will be price controls on energy and the introduction of some form of rent control. In recent UK political history, the less interventionist political parties have soon adopted the price-control proposals of the more interventionist parties, so the fact that the two main parties currently disagree on these two matters might turn out to be irrelevant.

The impact of price controls is not trivial, even if their effects can be masked by complex design and methods of implementation. For example, even the government believes that controls on prices in the finance sector could reduce competition. And a similar fear is so great in relation to the minimum pricing of alcohol that the measure may well be illegal. Maximum prices can have the effect of creating price stickiness so that competition does not lead to falling prices. In energy markets, companies can respond to the threat of future price freezes by buying energy in forward markets so that, if energy prices subsequently fall, companies will not be able to pass on the benefits to consumers. If so-called 'second-generation' rent controls are introduced, we might avoid the wholesale destruction of the rental market that happened between 1918 and 1988, but we cannot avoid the inevitable trade-off between the rent paid and quality of accommodation.

The impact of price controls is often most acutely felt by the least well off – though, it should be noted that many of the gainers might be on low incomes too. With regard to minimum wages, while some people may benefit from higher pay, others are likely to become unemployed. Their skills may then deteriorate so that their productivity falls further below the minimum wage level and short-term unemployment can turn into long-term unemployment.

Given that there can be so many problems arising from legislated price floors and ceilings, why are they ubiquitous?

The answer may well lie in the 'economics of politics' or 'public choice'. Organised interest groups often gain from price control: those interest groups might be incumbent firms that wish to see markets oligopolised because entry into markets becomes more difficult if prices are controlled. Certainly, once a control exists, it becomes difficult to remove because the losers from its removal can easily identify their losses while the gainers would be dispersed and may not realise that they could benefit from the removal of a price control. Also, politicians often like to gain approval from groups of voters who are, rationally, not well informed about economic issues and do not understand the second- and third-round effects of price regulation. If we are to change policy, we not only need to understand the effects of the policy, we also need to understand the political-economic process by which the policy came about.

This collection is very well timed, especially in the British context. The issues are being discussed widely and new proposals for price controls are brought forward with great regularity. The editors, both experts in the field of the study of markets, Christopher Coyne and Rachel Coyne, have put together chapters from leading authors that cover the subject to great effect. The authors examine the detailed problems of price control in their particular areas while explaining the basic concepts very effectively. The historical context is also given, together with an introduction to the basic economic ideas that is ideal for high school and first-year university students. As such, this publication makes an excellent contribution to the IEA's educational mission.

The views expressed in this monograph are, as in all IEA publications, those of the authors and not those of the Institute (which has no corporate view), its managing trustees, Academic Advisory Council members or senior staff. With some exceptions, such as with the publication of lectures, all IEA monographs are blind peer-reviewed by at least two academics or researchers who are experts in the field.

PHILIP BOOTH

Editorial and Programme Director
Institute of Economic Affairs
Professor of Insurance and Risk Management
Cass Business School, City University, London
March 2015

SUMMARY

- Price controls damage markets by preventing the supply of products rising to meet demand. They can cause significant welfare losses, a deterioration in product quality, a reduction in investment and, in the long run, higher prices. Price controls also encourage black markets and illegal economic activity.
- In the labour market, minimum wages can reduce employment. This is especially so among the most vulnerable groups. Minimum wages can also lengthen unemployment terms and create labour markets in which 'lucky' insiders gain at the expense of 'unlucky' outsiders.
- Rent controls in the UK were disastrous in terms of their effect on the private rented sector. In the period of control, the private rented sector fell from three quarters to one tenth of the total housing stock. Since liberalisation, private renting has rebounded to around one sixth of all housing provision.
- Although the form of rent control currently being proposed by politicians would not have the same devastating effects as the controls used in the 20th century, 'second-generation' rent controls would damage choice, reduce quality of accommodation, raise the costs of investment and hence could increase rents in the long run. Rent control is a typical example of the use of price control to suppress the symptoms of mistaken policies: fundamentally, the reason why the cost of housing is so high in the UK is because of highly restrictive

land-use planning laws. No attempt to reduce rents by regulation can alleviate this problem.

- The proposed freeze of energy prices comes after a number of years in which governments have been retreating from the policy of liberalisation which was very effective in reducing prices. Specifically, the energy regulator has reduced the number of tariffs that companies can offer and prevented some forms of discounting. One result has been higher profit margins for providers. In the short run, a pre-announced price freeze is likely to lead to higher prices as companies take action to raise the base level at which prices are frozen. In the long run, such interventions raise the cost of capital and are likely to reduce investment. We need to return, instead, to the policy of liberalisation that was so effective in creating competition and reducing prices.

- Price controls currently cover large parts of the rail sector. These controls benefit some rail travellers, though taxpayers and other rail travellers bear the costs. It is mistakenly assumed that there is a monopoly in rail travel when rail is simply one small part of a vibrant market for transport services. Fare caps artificially encourage overcrowding at peak times and on particular lines and reduce the incentive to invest in the network. They also prevent product differentiation in transport such as the development of low-cost, short-haul trains with more basic seating facilities or luxury commuter coaches.

- Until recently, UK financial products markets have been free of price controls for a number of decades. However, the government has recently brought in caps on the cost of short-term consumer finance (payday loans). The government had previously rejected such price control for good reasons. The evidence from overseas suggests that restricting consumer credit can drive the market underground or lead vulnerable consumers to complete financial breakdown and thus make all credit and financial services difficult to access in the future.

- The UK government is introducing controls on pensions charges. Again, this is happening after such controls were rejected and despite evidence that the market was working effectively. The government concedes that it is likely that price controls will inhibit new entry and competition in the industry. One government agency suggests that the price cap might become a 'target' for providers who might otherwise have priced their products lower than the cap. It is clear from the development of the charge capping agenda that the proposed regulation will be driven by political rather than economic considerations.

- Controls on university fees are very common around the world. However, the systems of student finance that governments have introduced prevent the competitive process operating in higher education that would otherwise help ensure that many students received a much lower cost education. The caps on fees, combined with the way student finance is provided, prevents a differentiated market developing which would provide different types of courses at different fee levels appropriate for a highly diverse student body.

- The Scottish government has passed legislation to implement a price floor in the market for alcohol. Such a measure remains under consideration in the rest of the UK. The health benefits of minimum pricing for alcohol are likely to be very small and the costs will be heavy and borne disproportionately by the low paid. It is likely that the main effect of minimum pricing will be that companies will move towards producing more expensive products and spending more on marketing. It is with good reason that the EU normally regards minimum price regulation as illegal.

TABLES AND FIGURES

1 INTRODUCTION

Christopher J. Coyne and Rachel L. Coyne

Introduction

Price controls refer to government-imposed restrictions on what can be charged for a good or service in the market. There are two types of price controls. A price ceiling restricts prices from exceeding a maximum price determined by government: an example would be rent controls of residential living spaces which set a legally mandated upper bound on the price that can be charged to tenants. A price floor, in contrast, prohibits the charging of prices below a predetermined minimum: an example would be a minimum wage law which sets a legal lower bound on what employers must pay employees.

The use of price controls by governments has a long history spanning thousands of years (see Schuettinger and Butler 1979). In ancient Rome, for instance, the government imposed price controls to attempt to combat inflation due to the debasement of currency. Operating under the belief that the inflation was due to speculation, in the year 301 Emperor Diocletian imposed price controls on a wide range of goods and services which were enforced by the threat of execution (see Bartlett 1994). The controls had a devastating impact on Rome's economy. In more recent times, government officials have continued to impose price controls to address a variety of social and economic issues. The US government imposed price controls during both world wars, as well as during the Korean War, with the goal of rationing items deemed as necessary by the government. Both the UK and US governments implemented general wage and price controls in the 1970s. In 1971, President Nixon famously imposed wage and price freezes for a ninety day period to combat inflation. The result was a series of unintended consequences including long queues for petrol and shortages of basic items, such as toilet paper, while inflation increased. And even though this example from the US is decades old, it is important to realise that government-imposed price controls are not a relic of the past.

One more recent illustrative case, which has received media attention, is that of Venezuela. The Venezuelan government has engaged in an ongoing experiment, which has lasted for over a decade, of imposing new and additional price controls on a wide array of goods and services to combat inflation and shortages. The result has been further shortages of basic items such as food and paper products, including toilet paper and disposable nappies. In general, the result of the price controls has been 'frequent product shortages and the emergence of a thriving black market. Some farmers and retailers are skirting the rules or have stopped selling certain goods altogether rather than sell them at a loss' (Millard and Gallegos 2006). The cost of these legally mandated controls has largely fallen on the backs of Venezuelan citizens, whose standards of living have been adversely affected.

In addition to the economic costs, price controls have led to increasing restrictions on the basic freedoms of Venezuelan citizens. For example, in response to the food shortages created by prior price controls, the government introduced a mandatory biometric tracking system in order to collect data on the purchases made by private citizens at supermarkets (see Rawlings 2014). The purpose of the system is to ensure that private citizens do not 'overbuy' key staples that are in short supply. The shortages that led to this system are the cumulative effect of numerous price controls, which have resulted in the micro-management of the daily lives and purchasing decisions of Venezuelans.

Although Venezuela is an extreme case in terms of the magnitude of government-imposed price controls, they are not alone in their use. Globally, the governments of countries of all income levels currently maintain an array of price controls on a wide variety of goods, services and factors of production, which typically include: education, energy, health care, labour, pharmaceuticals and water. As these examples show, price controls have long been used by governments in a variety of contexts to attempt to address various economic, social and political issues.

Moreover, there is every reason to believe that price controls will remain a politically viable policy option for the foreseeable future. To provide just one example, consider that on 25 September 2013, the *Financial Times* published an article titled, 'Labour leader Ed Miliband defends UK energy reform pledge' (Parker et al. 2013). The article discusses Miliband's proposed reforms, which include the introduction of energy price controls in the form of a 20-month freeze on gas and electricity prices. Miliband argues that his policy, if implemented, will address what he calls the 'cost of living crisis' in the UK.

Given the historical use of price controls, as well as continued calls for future price freezes, the crucial question is: are price controls an effective means to achieve the stated end of improving standards of living for a significant number of citizens? The purpose of this book is to analyse various aspects and applications of price controls to answer this question. Although the main focus of the chapters is on the situation in the UK, the underlying analysis is applicable to any case of price controls. The economic analysis of price controls is straightforward, yet typically neglected by policymakers and citizens, who are too often seduced by the heartwarming rhetoric associated with controlling prices in the name of improving living standards. The authors point out the direct and indirect effects of imposing legally mandated controls on prices which can be significant. At a minimum such controls distort economic activity and harm the dynamism of the market economy. At the extreme, such as in Venezuela, the imposition of price controls can have truly devastating effects on a country's economy, the costs of which tend to fall on private citizens.

The contributors to this book explore the various aspects of government-imposed price controls across a variety of different cases. In Chapter 2 we review the basic economics of price controls with an emphasis on both the seen and unseen costs of these policies. In the following chapter (Chapter 3), Robert Miller discusses four historical cases where governments implemented price controls with the goal of combating inflation. Among other things, his chapter demonstrates the frequency of price controls across different historical contexts, in this case over two millennia. Miller also discusses how, in each instance, price controls were ineffective in combatting inflation. The subsequent chapters apply the economic logic of price controls to an array of present-day situations in the UK.

Chapter 4, by Stanley Siebert, provides an analysis of wage controls in the form of minimum wages. The discussion in this chapter is especially relevant, since governments around the world maintain a variety of wage controls which distort labour markets and affect broader economic activity. Indeed, if anything, such controls are becoming more common. In the subsequent chapter (Chapter 5), Ryan Bourne analyses the flaws of rent ceilings, which are price controls intended to foster affordable living. Bourne makes the important distinction between 'first-generation' and 'second-generation' price controls. The former entails the implementation of a hard price ceiling, which prevents landlords from charging market rents. The latter is more complex and allows for some, government-approved, changes in rent, for example, when there are changes in tenants. Bourne's discussion explores the perverse economic effects of both forms of control.

Energy markets are yet another area where government-imposed price controls are prevalent. Colin Robinson offers an economic discussion of caps on energy prices in Chapter 6. In doing so he provides insight into the evolution of the UK market as government regulators have repeatedly attempted to influence and manipulate energy prices through price controls. In Chapter 7, Richard Wellings analyses the regulation of rail fares in Britain. He notes that even though the railway industry was privatised in the 1990s, the industry remains heavily influenced by government. The sources of government control include state subsidies, the mandated structure of the industry and controls on fares. His analysis traces the economic consequences of this pseudo privatisation with an emphasis on the interaction of these three types of government influence over the railway industry.

Financial markets play a crucial role in almost all economic activity, either directly or indirectly. These markets are also among the most heavily regulated by governments around the world. Given this, in Chapter 8, Philip Booth and Stephen Davies explore one important aspect of the government regulation of financial markets: the imposition of caps on interest rates and on the charges associated with financial products, such as pensions, in the UK. Their chapter accomplishes two important things. Firstly, pensions have been a neglected area of study by academics in the area of finance: their contribution remedies this gap in the literature. Secondly, in demonstrating the costs of price controls in one segment of the financial market, Booth and Davies provide a glimpse into the significant costs of government manipulation of broader financial markets which goes well beyond the caps they discuss.

Many countries are currently debating the best way to deal with the rising costs of higher education. One policy that is often proposed is the imposition of price controls to limit increases in these costs. In Chapter 9, Steven Schwartz discusses why university price controls are ineffective in achieving this goal. His analysis explores the structure of higher education in the UK and explains how the resulting incentives encourage behaviours that run counter to the stated goals of those who advocate for price controls to limit costs. Finally, in Chapter 10, Christopher Snowden analyses minimum unit pricing (MUP), a policy which imposes a price floor below which retailers cannot sell a unit of alcohol. His discussion explains why this policy is not effective in achieving the goals of its advocates, which include reducing excessive drinking and alcohol-related mortality, and why the predicted benefits of MUP are likely to be exaggerated.

Even this brief summary of the chapters that follows demonstrates why a book exploring the economics of price controls is necessary. The use of government-mandated price controls is ubiquitous both historically and in the present. The chapters that follow are a reminder that simple economics is by no means simple-minded economics. In stark contrast, the contributors to this volume demonstrate the power of basic economic analysis for understanding the full costs of public policies. It is our hope that this monograph will be of value to policymakers, citizens, and scholars, and that they will consider the seen and unseen costs of using price controls to address perceived policy problems. Given what is at stake in terms of human well-being, doing so is of the utmost importance.

References

Bartlett B. (1994) How excessive government killed ancient Rome. *Cato Journal* 14(2): 287–303.

Millard, P. and Gallegos, R. (2006) Price caps ail Venezuelan economy. *Wall Street Journal*, February 15. http://online.wsj.com/articles/SB 113997821637774456 (accessed 10 March 2015).

Parker, G., Rigby, E. and Pickard, J. (2013) Labour leader Ed Miliband defends UK energy reform pledge. *Financial Times*, 25 September.

Rawlings, C. G. (2014) Controversial fingerprinting machines rolled out in some Venezuelan stores. Reuters, 25 September. http://www

.reuters.com/article/2014/09/25/us-venezuela-food-idUSKCN0HK-2BY20140925 (accessed 10 March 2015).

Schuettinger, R. L. and Butler, E. F. (1979) *Forty Centuries of Wage and Price Controls: How Not to Fight Inflation*. Washington, DC: Heritage Foundation.

2   THE ECONOMICS OF PRICE CONTROLS

Christopher J. Coyne and Rachel L. Coyne

The crucial role of prices in solving the economic problem

Prices are a commonly misunderstood concept. Many view prices as random numbers assigned by a seller. Related to this, many see prices as being an impediment to accomplishing their desired goals. For example, a young adult may desire to live in central London but quickly realises that they cannot to do so given the relatively high price of renting a flat in that area. The view of prices as impediments to achieving one's goals is one reason why there are so often calls for politicians and regulators to place controls on prices. The belief, from the perspective of proponents of price controls, is that, if regulators impose controls, then people will be able to achieve goals that would otherwise be unachievable. For example, in order to assist younger citizens with their cost of living, a politician may propose some combination of rent controls and a living wage to make cities such as London more affordable. These views, however, misconstrue the fundamental nature and role that prices play in an economic system.

Prices are central to solving the core economic problem that all societies face: how are scarce resources to be (re)allocated to meet as many of the unlimited wants of consumers as possible? Answering this question is crucial for improving standards of living since the more consumer wants can be met, the better off people are. One of the main contributions of Nobel Laureate F. A.

Hayek (1945) was his clarification of the exact nature of the economic problem. He noted: 'The economic problem of society is ... not merely a problem of how to allocate "given" resources – if "given" is taken to mean given to a single mind which deliberately solves the problem set by these "data". It is rather a problem of ... the utilization of knowledge which is not given to anyone in its totality' (pages 519–20). Hayek's point is that economic interactions rely on dispersed knowledge, some of which exists for all to grasp but much of which is inarticulate, tacit knowledge that is difficult to make explicit and is not available to everyone (see Hayek 1945; Lavoie 1986). Such knowledge must be discovered through experience and experimentation (see Hayek 1978). Because tacit knowledge cannot be expressed in an objective manner, it is not 'out there' for others to obtain in the same way as articulated knowledge in books lining library shelves (see Lavoie 1985: 76–87; Boettke 2002). Part of the reason that markets are so effective in allocating resources is that they allow dispersed individuals to take advantage of the knowledge possessed by others to discover a solution to the economic problem. But how do markets do this?

At the core of the effectiveness of markets is the notion of 'economic calculation', which refers to the decision-making process of how to best allocate scarce resources among the array of feasible alternatives. Economic calculation refers to the determination of the expected value-added of a potential course of action. For example, should scarce steel be used to construct a new office building, school building, hospital or some other structure? Or should it sit idle because none of the possible alternatives are profitable given the cost of steel and other inputs? By comparing the relative expected value-added across feasible alternatives, decision makers are able to choose the course of action with the highest expected social return. Crucial to this decision-making process are money prices and profit-and-loss accounting.

Money prices, which serve as a common unit of calculation, capture the relative scarcity, or opportunity cost, of different goods based on context-specific conditions, and they communicate this information to others in the economy (see Mises 1920; Hayek 1945; Thomsen 1992). This is powerful precisely because people are able to act on the context-specific knowledge reflected in prices without needing to actually possess any specific insight into the actual local conditions. For example, if a loaf of organic bread from a local baker costs £1.50, this reflects the costs of production and distribution of the bread (including the value of the time of the assistant serving in the shop) as well as reflecting the demand for organic bread relative to alternatives by other consumers. It is not necessary for the buyer to know anything about the baker's preferences for leisure versus working, how or why the ingredients cost the amount they do, or why other consumers may be willing to pay more for organic bread than other types of bread. Nor is it necessary for potential suppliers who are thinking of entering the market to know these things. This information is reflected in prices in a freely functioning economy.

The economist Thomas Sowell (1980) effectively captures this point when he writes: 'Prices are important not because money is considered paramount but because prices are a fast and effective conveyor of information through a vast society in which fragmented knowledge must be coordinated' (page 80). This information is crucial because it allows people to compare the prices of inputs, which reflect underlying scarcity conditions, to the expected profitability of numerous alternatives, all of which are technologically feasible (see Hoff 1981; Boettke 1998; Horwitz 1996, 1998). The resulting profit or loss – the difference between the cost of production and the sales price – provides feedback as to whether this estimate was accurate or not. A profit indicates that resources have been combined in a manner that generates value to others, while a loss signals the opposite: it signals that resources could have been allocated to a higher-valued use that would increase welfare. A simple example will illustrate this logic.

Consider a scenario in which an entrepreneur produces a new product for a cost of £25 and sells it for a price £50. What does this £25 profit indicate? There are many other things that the producer could have made using the resources that cost him £25. Some would have led to a loss while others would have led to a smaller profit. The profit of £25 indicates that consumers value the good produced more than the alternatives that could have been produced with those same resources. This profit signals to the producer, as well as to other entrepreneurs, that they have allocated resources in a manner that consumers value relative to the alternatives and encourages them to supply more. A loss signals that consumers do not value the current allocation of resources. The loss provides an incentive for entrepreneurs to adjust by reallocating scarce resources to other uses.

This ongoing process has several effects. The profit will tend to draw other entrepreneurs into the market who will seek to capture customers by charging a lower price. Another important effect is that entrepreneurs face constant pressure to come up with new and cheaper means of producing the good so as to increase their profit. If they cut production costs from £25 to £20, they keep these savings as additional profit – though other producers will then be attracted into the market so that prices may then fall. The result is ever-present competition and innovation, which benefit consumers since producers must adjust to meet their demands in order to remain profitable.

It is the information and incentive provided by monetary prices and profit-and-loss accounting that makes markets so effective in solving the economic problem. The process of economic calculation guides market participants in adapting their plans and reallocating resources to new and more highly valued uses to maximise the well-being of consumers. The lure of profit incentivises innovation, and prices guide innovators in determining which projects are feasible and which are not. Mistakes are, of course, frequently made, but markets provide the information and incentives to adapt accordingly.

Economic calculation is especially crucial as the production of goods and services becomes increasingly complex, which is a defining characteristic of economic progress and an advanced economic system. The economist Don Lavoie (1985) captures this point when he writes: 'price information represents knowledge about a continually and rapidly changing structure of economic relationships' (page 82). To understand this point, consider the complexity involved in the production of what is typically considered by those in developed countries to be a basic good – a toaster.

Thomas Thwaites (2014), a London-based designer, embarked on a fascinating project, the 'Toaster Project', in which he attempted to build a simple toaster by hand and from scratch. He quickly found that the project was an extremely complicated one. The toaster required copper, iron, nickel, mica and plastic, all of which Thwaites had to obtain from mines and other sources in a variety of geographical locations. After much travel and effort to extract and process the necessary materials, he constructed his (extremely ugly) toaster, which proceeded, upon being plugged into an electric socket, to burn out in a matter of seconds. His project is a perfect illustration of the importance of economic calculation as indicated by his realisation that 'the scale of industry involved in making a toaster is ridiculous but at the same time the chain of discoveries and small technological developments that occurred along the way make it entirely reasonable' (2014). This chain of events was guided by the feedback provided by economic calculation coupled with the adaptability of markets. The result is that toasters are readily available to consumers when they want them at a relatively low price.

Further adding to the sheer complexity of advanced economies is the importance of what economists call complementary goods: goods and services that are consumed together. For example, cars require petrol, spare parts, repair equipment and trained mechanics in order to operate. Just like the construction of a basic toaster, most people living in relatively wealthy societies take the wide array of complementary goods available for granted. However, when one considers the level of coordination required for each of these various complementary goods not only to be produced but to be available and waiting when needed by consumers, these taken-for-granted goods and services are truly amazing phenomena. Someone, somewhere, has to anticipate the need for these complementary goods and services and make them available to consumers on demand.

In markets, consumers do not submit a master wish list to a central planner who then allocates resources accordingly. Instead, prices and profit-and-loss accounting guide entrepreneurs in discovering a (new) solution to the economic problem by producing and innovating existing and new goods and services that consumers value. This process is the essence of broader economic progress as resources are reallocated, on an ongoing basis, to their highest-valued, welfare-maximizing use. It is precisely the fact that no one is in charge that makes markets so flexible and effective. Each individual who possesses unique skills and knowledge is able to engage in experimentation and discovery that benefits not only themselves but others as well. Market prices link individuals and markets together by communicating a vast amount of information. The lure of profit and fear of loss incentivise people to continually adjust their behaviour. Given this understanding of the market process and the central role played by prices, we are now in a position to understand the consequences of imposing price controls. The next section illustrates the market process described above, as well as the effect of price controls.

Illustrating the market process and the distortionary effects of price controls

The market process described above can be illustrated using a basic supply and demand framework as illustrated in Figure 1. The downward-sloping demand curve, 'D', represents the reality that, all else constant, consumers are willing to purchase a greater quantity of a good or service the lower the price of each unit. Likewise, the upward-sloping supply curve, 'S', represents the reality that, all else constant, producers are willing to supply a greater quantity of a good or service the higher the price they receive per unit.

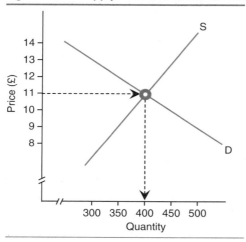

Figure 1   The supply and demand framework

The intersection of the market supply and demand curve represents an equilibrium price and quantity where the amount demanded by consumers is exactly equal to the amount supplied by producers. Of course, in reality, this equilibrium point is never actually reached due to changing conditions on both sides of the market. However, this basic framework is useful in that it illustrates how markets and prices operate.

Consider what happens when the price is above the hypothetical equilibrium price. Assume, for instance, that the price is £13 instead of the equilibrium price of £11. At a price of £13 the quantity supplied by producers is 450 while the quantity demanded by consumers is 300. In other words, at a price of £13 there is a surplus of 150 units because the quantity supplied (450) is greater than the quantity demanded (300). The result will be downward pressure on the price as producers realise that their surplus inventory will remain unsold at a price of £13. As suppliers lower the price, consumers are willing to purchase more of the good and less will be supplied. This process continues until the surplus is eroded.

The reverse happens when the price is below the hypothetical equilibrium price. Consider a scenario in which the price is £9. At this price the quantity supplied is 350 units, while the quantity demanded is 500 units, resulting in a shortage of 150 units. At a price of £9, consumers demand more than producers are willing to supply, resulting in a shortage. In the face of a shortage, there will be upward pressure on the market price as consumers bid up the price of the existing goods. This process will continue until the price rises to £11, where the quantity supplied is equal to the quantity demanded.

The basic supply and demand framework highlights the fact that, in an unhampered market, there is an inherent tendency for prices to adjust to align the different interests of consumers and suppliers. This is an ongoing and continual process, which is precisely why unhindered prices are so important. As discussed in the previous section, prices capture the context-specific realities facing individual economic actors. These individuals do not have to have any working knowledge of economics or the market process but they act as if they do precisely because prices provide information and profit and loss provides the incentive to act on that information.

It now becomes clear why price controls are a problem. From an economic standpoint, price controls are problematic because they distort the price mechanism's ability to allocate resources to their highest-valued uses through voluntary exchange. In unhampered markets, prices work to coordinate supplies and the demands of consumers and ration existing resources efficiently.

By legally manipulating the market price, price controls distort this process by preventing mutually beneficial exchanges which would have otherwise occurred in the absence of the legal restriction. Figures 2 and 3 illustrate the direct distortions resulting from the implementation of price controls.

Figure 2 A price floor

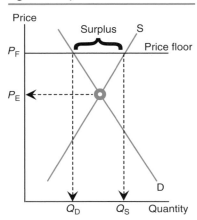

A price floor is a legally mandated price that is set above the equilibrium price. The government mandated price is illustrated by the solid line (P_F) in Figure 2. As discussed above, a price above the equilibrium price (P_E) will result in a surplus, where suppliers produce more than consumers demand ($Q_S > Q_D$). In the unhampered market, the price would fall to erode the surplus. However, suppliers are unable to lower their price, by law, below the mandated price floor. The result is that the surplus persists.

To provide an illustration of this logic, suppose that the market for labour is coordinated through genuine market prices. In this case supply and demand will tend to be brought into balance. Now suppose the government imposes a price floor in the form of a minimum wage, above the equilibrium price, with the goal of improving standards of living of low-skilled workers. At the artificially high price, the quantity of labour supplied will exceed the quantity of labour demanded, resulting in a surplus of labour. In other words, some workers who want to work at the artificially high price will be unable to find employment and people who want work doing will be unable to find people to do the work even though, without the legal price floor, there would be willing workers.

A price ceiling is a legally mandated price that is set below the equilibrium price. This legally mandated ceiling is illustrated by the solid line (P_C) in Figure 3. As discussed, a price below the equilibrium price (P_E) will result in a shortage where consumers demand more than producers are willing to supply ($Q_D > Q_S$). In the unhampered market, the price would rise to remove this shortage. However, consumers are legally unable to raise their offer price and sellers are unable to legally raise their price above the mandated price ceiling. The result is that the shortage persists.

Figure 3   A price ceiling

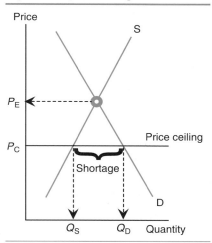

To provide an example of this dynamic, consider an unhampered market in energy where supply and demand is balanced by the free-functioning price mechanism. If the government imposes a price ceiling below the market price, the quantity of energy supplied will fall, while the quantity of energy demanded will increase. The result will be a shortage of energy. Some consumers will wish to buy energy, be willing to pay the cost to suppliers but it will be illegal for them to do so. There is a genuine welfare loss here.[1]

It is important to note that price controls do not make everyone worse off. Those who are able to secure goods at the artificially low price – in the case of a price ceiling – or those who are lucky enough to obtain a higher price for their services – in the

---

1   For another, classic, illustration of this logic, see Friedman and Stigler (1946).

case of a price floor – are made better off. At the same time, those who are unable to secure the good they desire at the artificially low price or those who are unable to find a buyer for their goods at the artificially higher price are made worse off because of the price control.

It should also be noted that all sorts of subtle processes do not take place when there is a price floor. For example, when there is a price floor on rents, people have less incentive to economise on the amount of accommodation they use if they are the lucky ones who can obtain a flat or house. As a result, price floors can lead to markets with 'insiders' and 'outsiders' with the lucky insiders having plentiful supply at a cheap price and others unable to obtain the good or service at all. Another important effect is that artificially capping prices can prevent the dynamics of the market operating in such a way that can bring forth new supply or bring about innovation to reduce demand. Imagine, for example, if there had been a price cap on oil as its price was increasing in the early 21st century. This would have reduced the incentive to research into new ways to exploit fossil fuels (such as shale gas fracking) and to conserve fuel and would have reduced investment in exploration. Exploration has the potential to move the supply curve out and new methods of conservation have the potential to move the demand curve to the left. These dynamics can then reduce prices below the floor. Without these dynamic market adjustments in uncontrolled markets, price ceilings, shortages and quality reductions may become permanent features of the market. In general, price controls generate a host of other costs which are often unseen and, therefore, overlooked.

Some overlooked costs of price controls

In addition to the direct and observable effects of price controls – shortages and surpluses – there is also a series of subsequent, indirect costs which emerge. Perhaps the best source for understanding these overlooked costs is to look to those who were directly involved in designing and implementing past controls. One such individual, G. Jackson Grayson Jr, served as the chairman of the Price Commission in the United States under President Nixon from 1971 to 1973. In this role Grayson was responsible for overseeing the implementation and enforcement of Nixon's price controls. After leaving his post, Grayson (1974) wrote: '[a]s a result of my sixteen months as price controller, I can list seven ways that controls interfere (negatively) with the market system and hasten its metamorphosis into a centralized economy' (page 10). Grayson's list can be paraphrased and summarised as follows.

Price controls distort economic activity

Price controls distort the allocation of resources both directly and indirectly. As discussed in the previous section, the direct effect is to create persistent shortages or surpluses while reducing the number of mutually beneficial exchanges that would have otherwise occurred in the absence of controls. But the implementation of price controls leads to a series of subsequent, indirect distortions as well, as people respond rationally to the immediate and direct effects of the controls.

In the absence of the ability to use prices to ration scarce goods, alternative mechanisms emerge. For example, shortages lead to queues resulting from excess demand for the good or service in question. This dynamic was evident in the centrally planned economies of Eastern Europe as well as in the US in the 1970s when the government imposed price controls on petrol. Long queues tend to lead to subsequent government interventions with rationing schemes. For example, the US government reacted to long queues for petrol by limiting consumer purchases of petrol to every second day.

The emergence of crime and black markets are another indirect negative effect of price controls. Unable to adjust prices legally, producers and buyers may move into the extralegal market to engage in exchange. Others, desperate to obtain goods for which there is a shortage, may engage in theft to obtain goods. To provide one illustration of black market activities, consider the case of farmers in the UK in World War II. Facing wartime meat rationing, many farmers under-reported animal births to the Ministry of Food and then sold the additional meat in the black market.

Yet another indirect effect of price controls is evasion, which can take on a variety of forms. For example, facing a price ceiling, sellers may charge additional fees or tie-ins to compensate for the fact that prices are required to be artificially low. There is also likely to be deterioration in the quality of the product or service. This may include the substitution of low-quality for high-quality ingredients in the production of a good or, in the case of rent controls, maintenance and investment not being carried out and poor-quality conditions being allowed to develop in accommodation.

Finally, a legal mandate on prices lowers the cost of buyers and sellers using non-monetary criteria – e.g. race, gender, religion, etc. – to allocate resources. Price floors will allow buyers to indulge their non-monetary preferences while price ceilings will allow sellers to do so. Consider an example of each to illustrate this. A minimum wage, which is a price floor, will create an excess supply – i.e. a surplus – of potential employees willing to work at the legally mandated wage. In this case employers, the buyers of labour, can indulge their non-monetary preferences in deciding who to hire. For example, they may decide to discriminate against a certain group or type of person in making their hiring decisions. Due to the price control, they are able to indulge these preferences precisely because there is a surplus of potential employees from which to choose.

Now consider the case of a rent control: a price ceiling. In this case there will be an excess demand – i.e. a shortage – for flats, which means that sellers can indulge their non-monetary preferences in choosing among potential tenants. Precisely because the price control creates an excess demand, landlords can discriminate and indulge their preferences without suffering a monetary cost for doing so. Turning away certain potential tenants based on non-monetary characteristics does not hurt the landlord because other potential tenants remain due to the artificially low price.

Price controls mask real changes to economic fundamentals

Price controls are often implemented with the goal of fighting inflation. But this, incorrectly, assumes that all wage-price increases are the result of inflation. In an unhampered market economy, there are constant, genuine changes to supply and demand conditions that will often lead to real price increases and relative price increases. The existence of price controls distorts the ability of the price mechanism to communicate this information by treating all price changes as if they are the result of inflation. The result is that scarce resources will not be reallocated to meet changes in the real, underlying economic conditions. Thus, due to persistent resource misallocations, standards of living will suffer.

During a period of price controls, the role of profit is neglected, if not entirely ignored

Initial calls for price controls – whether from the public or from policymakers – are often justified on the grounds of profits for certain industries being 'too high'. By implementing price controls, the logic follows, the government can limit profits while passing savings on to consumers. The implementation of controls reinforces the, incorrect, sentiment that profits come at the expense of consumers as opposed to the actual reality that profits flow from the successful satisfaction of consumer wants.

Moreover, the implementation of controls discourages long-term investments due to the artificially low prices and a weakened profit motive. We noted above how quality deterioration under price controls will affect customers in the short term as producers respond to the implementation of controls. However, this is only part of the story, as quality deterioration will also affect consumers over the long term. In the face of price controls, suppliers will have a disincentive to invest in either expanding production or improving the quality of the controlled good in future periods. Indeed, the full impact of price controls may not be felt for many years and then become disconnected in the minds of policymakers from the original policy, so that there is little political pressure to reverse the controls. In general, supply is more elastic in the long than in the short run. An energy price control, for example, may lead to a relatively small reduction in supply immediately because the short-run marginal cost of production of energy may be lower than the controlled price. However, the long-run marginal cost will be higher than the short-run marginal cost because the continued production of energy involves investment in new plant and equipment. That new investment might not be forthcoming in the controlled market. This is also problematic precisely because new investment would lower the price of energy in the future, the very end that proponents of price controls claim that they are seeking.

Thus, during control periods, the role of profits in rewarding producers for supplying a good that consumers value is weakened if not altogether removed. This discourages increased future production, which only exacerbates the initial perceived problem of 'too little' supply at 'too high' a price.

Price controls replace market competition with political competition

The implementation of price controls does not change the fundamental nature of the economic problem. Decisions still need to be made about how to best allocate scarce resources among an array of feasible alternatives. In the absence of price controls, these decisions are made through the market process, which relies on true market prices reflecting the relative scarcity of resources. However, with the implementation of controls, the market process is distorted and political competition, at least partly, replaces market competition. Efforts are shifted from pleasing private consumers to attempting to influence the political process, which ultimately determines how controls are implemented and enforced. The result is that price controls attract an array of political interests who seek to use controls for their own narrow pursuits at the expense of the broader interests of private consumers. As Grayson (1974) writes, 'wage-price controls provide a convenient stone for those who have economic and political axes to grind, particularly those interested in promoting a centralized economic system' (page 11).

Price controls normalise attitudes of reliance on government

Price controls threaten the dynamism of markets, which rely on profit and loss to operate effectively. In the absence of controls, those in business must weigh the perceived risk and reward of alternative courses of action. Misjudgment by entrepreneurs results in losses and, at the extreme, bankruptcy. However, price controls change the decision-making calculus of entrepreneurs. Instead of having to weigh the true costs and benefits of their actions, entrepreneurs come to see government regulators as a potential source of economic security that can insulate them from the often harsh realities of competitive markets. The result is that '[t]he controlled become dependent on the controllers and want regulations continued in preference to the competition of the dynamic market' (Grayson 1974: 12). The cumulative effect is the replacement of profit and loss as the mechanism for determining winners and losers with an increasing reliance on political authorities for protection from the realities of consumer-driven market competition. Thus, the voices of private consumers are weakened as is the incentive for businesses to make consumer satisfaction a priority.

Price controls generate regime uncertainty

The implementation of price controls gives regulators the power to shape economic outcomes. In the unhampered market, businesspeople must attempt to forecast accurately the wants of consumers. Price controls add another element of uncertainty into the process. Now businesspeople must not only anticipate what their customers want but also forecast how regulators will act. This creates 'regime uncertainty', which refers to ambiguity surrounding the protection of property and the stability of rules and regulations in the future (see Higgs 1997). If businesspeople are uncertain about future regulations and controls, their ability to plan and forecast is hampered, which raises the cost of planning and investing. Further, entrepreneurs must shift at least part of their focus to attempting to anticipate what regulators will do in the future. This shift comes at the expense of private consumers who would otherwise be the main focus of for-profit business.

Price controls mask the true causes of economic problems

Price controls are typically framed as a response to some supposed market failure. In this scenario, government regulators are seen as the quick-fix solution to perceived problems inherent in markets, which are often, incorrectly, blamed on such things as 'speculation' and 'hoarding'. This overly simplified framing masks the true underlying cause of economic ills. In an environment of high inflation, for example, calls for government-imposed price controls completely neglect the role of monetary policy as a fundamental cause of inflation. In the case of wage controls, a minimum wage may raise the pay for some individuals while leaving other individuals unemployed. The policy may well, in effect, be masking the effects of low productivity caused, for example, by defective education policy. The low levels of productivity will manifest themselves in the form of higher unemployment rather than in the form of lower wages. The ultimate result is that price controls mislead private citizens regarding both the fundamental causes of perceived economic problems and the solutions to address those problems.

Conclusion

It is not hard to see why price controls are appealing. They offer what appears to be a quick and simple solution to rising prices and allow policymakers to provide short-term benefits to certain groups of people. It is true, by definition, that price controls will either raise (in the case of a price floor) or lower (in the case of a price ceiling) the price of the good or service in question. Further, it is true that not all people are made worse off by the implementation of price controls. Under a price floor, those who receive a higher price for their good or service than they would have in the absence of the control are made better off. Likewise, under a price ceiling, those who pay a lower price for a good or service than they otherwise would have are made better off. Economics, however, indicates that price controls are far from costless, and the associated costs are far reaching and potentially significant.

As we have emphasised, there are both direct and indirect costs to price control policies. While some of these costs are seen (such as a shortage or surplus) many are unseen: for example, long-term investments that would have taken place in the absence of controls may no longer take place because investors fear they will not be able to make an adequate return on their investment. When one appreciates the complexity of the market system, it becomes evident that understanding the full consequences of a price control is very difficult. What is clear is that price controls set in motion a series of unintended consequences as producers and consumers respond to the new incentives created by the introduction of controls. More often than not, these unintended consequences exacerbate the very problem that proponents of controls claim to correct.

The logic of the seen and unseen also helps to explain why, given the costs associated with price controls, they continue to remain popular among politicians and much of the public. Price controls are readily observable – i.e. seen – in that the public can readily observe the legally mandated price set by government. Given the difficulty of understanding and tracing the unseen consequences discussed throughout this chapter, it appears to many that these controls are pure benefit with little to no cost. But the economic way of thinking indicates this is wrongheaded. As Thomas Sowell (2007) writes, '[e]conomists have long been saying that there is no free lunch but politicians get elected by promising free lunches. Controlling prices creates the illusion of free lunches.' Furthermore, price controls are a low-cost method for politicians to reward interest groups for their support at the ballot box. For example, in some countries, advocating higher minimum wage laws is a well-known method for politicians to reward unions for supporting their election efforts.

If the goal of policymakers is to improve standards of living, policy must focus on incentivising improved quality and availability. This is accomplished by creating an environment conducive to economic freedom and contestable markets where entrepreneurs can experiment and subject their conjectures to the market test. Price controls undermine economic freedom and, therefore, must be dismissed as a means for improving standards of living. The reality is that price controls harm the well-being of many while providing political gains to the few. Until the economics of price controls is appreciated, legally mandated prices will remain a viable policy option despite their historical failure and the significant costs that they impose on the average citizen, who suffers under such policies.

References

Bartlett, B. (1994) How excessive government killed ancient Rome. *Cato Journal* 14(2): 287–303.

Boettke, P. J. (1998) Economic calculation: the Austrian contribution to political economy. *Advances in Austrian Economics* 5: 131–58.

Boettke, P. J. (2002) Information and knowledge: Austrian economics in search of its uniqueness. *Review of Austrian Economics* 15(4): 263–74.

Friedman, M. and Stigler, G. (1946) *Roofs or Ceilings? The Current Housing Problem.* Irvington-on-Hudson, NY: The Foundation for Economic Education.

Grayson, C. J. (1974) Controls are not the answer. *Challenge*, November–December.

Hayek, F. A. (1945) The use of knowledge in society. *American Economic Review* 35(4): 519–30.

Hayek, F. A. (1978) Competition as a discovery procedure. In *New Studies in Philosophy, Politics, Economics, and the History of Ideas* (ed. F. A. Hayek). Chicago, IL: University of Chicago Press.

Higgs, R. (1997) Regime uncertainty: why the Great Depression lasted so long and why prosperity resumed after the war. *Independent Review* 1(4): 561–90.

Hoff, T. J. B. (1981) *Economic Calculation in the Socialist Society.* Indianapolis, IN: Liberty Fund.

Horwitz, S. (1996) Money, money prices, and the Socialist calculation debate. *Advances in Austrian Economics* 3: 59–77.

Horwitz, S. (1998) Monetary calculation and Mises's critique of planning. *History of Political Economy* 30(3): 427–50.

Lavoie, D. (1985) *National Economic Planning: What Is Left?* Cambridge, MA: Ballinger Publishing Company.

Lavoie, D. (1986) The market as a procedure for discovery and conveyance of inarticulate knowledge. *Comparative Economic Studies* 28(1): 1–19.

Mises, L. von. (1920 [1935]) Economic calculation in the Socialist commonwealth. In *Collectivist Economic Planning* (ed. F. A. Hayek). London: Routledge.

Parker, G., Rigby, E. and Pickard, J. (2013) Labour leader Ed Miliband defends UK energy reform pledge. *Financial Times*, 25 September.

Schuettinger, R. L. and Butler, E. F. (1979) *Forty Centuries of Wage and Price Controls: How Not to Fight Inflation*. Washington, DC: Heritage Foundation.

Sowell, T. (1980) *Knowledge and Decisions*. New York: Basic Books.

Sowell, T. (2007) Pricing 101. *National Review Online*, 21 February. http://www.nationalreview.com/article/220039/pricing-101-thomas-sowell (accessed 10 March 2015).

Thomsen, E. F. (1992) *Prices and Knowledge: A Market-Process Perspective*. New York: Routledge.

Thwaites, T. (2014) The toaster project. http://www.thetoasterproject.org/page2.htm (accessed 10 March 2015).

3 PRICE CEILINGS: ANCIENT AND MODERN

Robert C. B. Miller

Taking low inflation for granted

Many price ceilings are understandable only in the light of inflation. Inflation does not currently appear to be the major problem it used to be. Over the last ten years, inflation in the UK has been only 2.7 per cent a year on average (2004–13). Hence it is worth reviewing how and why some representative inflations have developed and why governments have tried so often and so unsuccessfully to mitigate the effects with price controls and price ceilings. It is only possible to examine the logic and the temptation of such controls in the circumstances which gave rise to them. This means examining why governments give way to the allure of inflation despite the damage that it does. In turn this will help explain why governments have resorted to price controls as a means of mitigating the consequences of the inflation they have unleashed.

In what follows we take the examples of four historic inflations and the price and wage ceilings which they provoked. These are not the only examples we could have taken, but they are sufficiently divided in time and type that any conclusions drawn may have broad application. In particular they took place in different times and places and had different proximate causes. The selected inflations and the price controls they provoked are: the inflation in the Roman Empire which culminated in Diocletian's Edict; the inflation of Weimar Germany; the Nazi Inflation before and during World War II; and the British inflation and experiments with wage and price controls between the 1940s and the 1970s.

The Great Roman Inflation

The Roman Empire founded by Augustus (Heath 2006) at the end of the Roman civil wars suffered from chronic inflation and, under the Emperor Diocletian, inflation accelerated sharply, provoking one of the earliest attempts to contain inflation by means of direct controls. Inflation in the ancient world was dissimilar from the forms it can take today as it was primarily currency depreciation. In other words, the issuers of the currency increased the supply by reducing the precious metal content. There seems to have been no equivalent of inflation being caused in the modern way through a fractional reserve banking system, where an increase in bank reserves can cause an increase in the money supply. Such was the Roman Empire from the first century to the fourth century. Inflation first trotted then changed to a canter before accelerating to a hyper-inflationary gallop under the Emperor Diocletian at the end of the third century.

The explanation for the Great Roman Inflation is much the same as for later inflations. The Roman Empire's initial success and apparent military and economic stability were the result of largely benign conditions on the empire's eastern and western frontiers. The early empire reached a state of uneasy equilibrium. Thus the attempt to create a new province between the Rhine and the Elbe proved impossible after the destruction of three legions in the Battle of the Teutoburg forest in 9 AD. On the other hand the conquest of most of Britain was achieved following Claudius's invasion in 43 AD. Frontier adjustments were evidently the result of nice judgements of military and economic advantage. There was no point in acquiring territory if it cost more to hold than the revenue it generated. Such adjustments included lowland

Scotland, occupied under Antoninus Pius for twenty years between 142 AD and 162 AD and the contested area between the Rhine and the Danube, which formed the mature continental European frontier of the empire.

An interesting (earlier) example of the unstable military–economic equilibrium of the Roman Empire in its high tide of the first century is the fate of Agricola's attempt to conquer Scotland in 80 AD. A legionary fortress at Inchtuthill was established in Perthshire to dominate the glens to the north. But because of a crisis in Moesia caused by an invasion by the Dacians, one of the legions occupying Britain (*Leg II Audiatrix*) had to be withdrawn (86 AD). The result was that the ambitious plan to subdue Scotland had to be abandoned and the fortress was demolished. The significance of this story is that the military and economic resources of the Roman Empire were limited and even in its heyday it was unable to both subdue Scotland and manage a crisis in Eastern Europe at the same time. Even at the best of times, the existence of the Roman Empire was somewhat precarious (Ward-Perkins 2005).

This unstable equilibrium helps explain the early Roman Empire's steadily accelerating inflation. Taxation was often high and random in its effects. The economic historian Rostovtzeff records the devastation caused to a province when a Roman army passed through it even when the empire was at its most secure (and aggressive) under Trajan (Rostovtzeff 1957: 355ff). With limited resources available to meet each crisis, the easiest course was to finance the necessary additional spending by currency depreciation. Coinage was issued with a lower precious metal content with the same nominal value (see Figure 4).

But why did the depreciation of the currency increase so rapidly? According to Professor Peter Heath (2006), two developments led to increased military and economic stress and, it would appear, to inflation. The first development was an agricultural revolution among the German tribes beyond the European

Figure 4   Roman currency depreciation between 64 and 273 AD

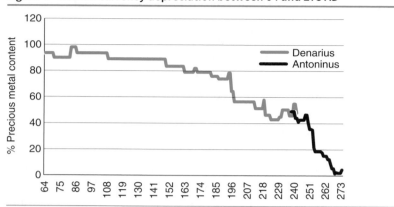

frontiers of the empire. This had a profound effect on their military capacity – and hence their ability to threaten the Roman provinces.

The second development was the creation of a Persian superpower in the third century on the eastern frontier of the Roman Empire. From around 230 AD the Sassanian dynasty formed Persia into a military superpower to rival the Roman Empire. In combination these developments posed threats to which the Roman Empire had no answer. The result was stretched resources and a gradually increasing use of currency depreciation to finance the necessary military spending.

A third development contributing to the stress on the economy of the Roman Empire was the 'Crisis of the Third Century' when, between 235 and 284 AD, emperor succeeded emperor in a series of usurpations. Between 258 and 274 AD, the empire split into three parts: Gaul, Britain and Spain forming one state; Syria, Palestine and Egypt forming another; the rest formed a rump state. The empire was only reunited by Aurelian in 274 AD. These tensions created a background of economic chaos, which led to the inflation illustrated in Figure 4.

Diocletian's price controls

Diocletian's famous edict of 301 AD was designed to contain inflation and reinforce the effect of a re-coinage. The full text of the edict has not been found. But enough is known to reveal the following. The death penalty was imposed for breaches of the controls and maximum prices were fixed for over 1,000 items. These included food, clothing, weekly wages and the price of transport by sea. There were reports of merchants withdrawing goods from sale. Diocletian combined his price controls with a reform of the currency. He established a new gold and silver coinage but continued to increase the copper coinage. The result was that the reduction in inflation was minimal.

The ancient world had no understanding of economic theory beyond the everyday understanding that good harvests meant low prices of foodstuffs. The Greeks and Romans also had no understanding of the concept of an economy – the aggregation and analysis of economic activity in a particular geographical area. As Finley explains, it is impossible to translate the title of Alfred Marshall's book *The Principles of Economics* into Latin or Greek (Finley 1973: 21). This was not an intellectual failing but a conceptual one. The necessary concepts only emerged, as Finley points out, in the mid 18th century. It should thus be no surprise that the inflation and Diocletian's Edict were seen as the result of the unchecked greed of merchants. Since there was no economic theory, there could be no economic explanation. Diocletian's fury is an example of the natural reaction of people untainted by theory and faced with untoward economic events.

The Weimar Inflation

What could be more different from the fall of the Western Roman Empire than the hyperinflation that beset Germany after World War I? There are, though, underlying similarities. The Weimar inflation was the result of the German government calling on resources which it could not acquire through taxation. One serious difficulty was that the German Empire had a tripartite system of national, state and municipal taxation, which made it difficult to increase taxes easily (Bresciani-Turroni 1968: 48).

Putting the Weimar Inflation in historical context, the German Empire had been far less successful than the allied powers in financing its huge war expenditures by taxation and genuine debt rather than money creation. Thus by 1919 only 12.5 per cent of total war expenditure had been met by taxation. No less than 26 per cent had been met by increases in short-term debt that had to be continually refinanced (Bresciani-Turroni 1968: 47). It was calculated that, between 1914 and 1923, only 15 per cent of government spending, which had been much increased by the war, had been financed by taxation (Bresciani-Turroni 1968: 74).

After the war, the government of the new republic was unable to carry out the fiscal retrenchment that the victorious powers were able to achieve. The position was complicated by a number of other factors. First Germany had lost territory and population, for example, Alsace and Lorraine to France and large territories in the east to the new state of Poland. As a result the tax base was reduced. Further, the 1919 Versailles peace imposed large reparations, which had to be met by the German government.

But the occupation of the Rhineland in early 1923 completely destroyed Germany's fiscal stability. The government made no attempt to raise taxes to meet the deficiency and relied on money creation to meet the costs of the passive resistance to the occupation. The German government lost revenues from coal, foreign trade duties and railway receipts. In addition spending on subsidies to the Ruhr industries increased. The result was hyperinflation (see Figure 5).

Throughout the whole inflationary period beginning in 1914, the German government had sought to mitigate inflation by price controls. These included controls on the price of bread, rents and railway rates. And these were combined with subsidies. Thus, at the end of 1922 just before the hyperinflation entered its extreme phase, rents amounted to only 0.4 per cent of (three-person) family incomes (Bresciani-Turroni 1968: 132ff). Indeed railway travel became so cheap that it was one of the very few luxuries which German people could enjoy at the worst of times (Guttman and Meehan 1975).

At the time, German economics was heavily influenced by the German institutional school, which ascribed little significance to the money supply and considered inflation an 'historical process'. Many, if not most, contemporary explanations of the inflation centred on the weakness of the exchange rate, which it was argued was caused by reparations and the resulting balance of payments deficit.

Figure 5   The Weimar Inflation

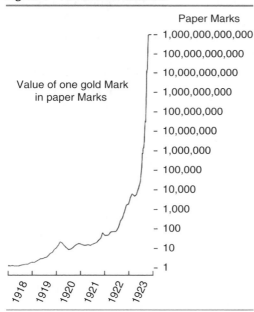

The Nazi Inflation

The dystopian Nazi state had the elements of other inflations and control regimes in such extreme form that they illustrate the syndrome with great clarity. Driven by a bizarre ideology wielded by a charismatic personality, the Nazi state sought to achieve a dominant position in Europe and the world from a position of perceived (and actual) weakness. Germany's economic weakness was such that, at every step, Hitler's career in office was beset by incipient economic crises (Tooze 2007). Thus, following the Munich triumph of 1938, the German economy was at a crisis point with threatening inflation and balance-of-payments crises.

The cause of Germany's economic problems was the rearmament programme, which meant that the state was seeking more resources than were available to it. This could not be achieved even with high rates of taxation – Germany was already one of the most highly taxed countries in Europe. Further, private consumption was cut to the bone. Private mortgages were forbidden from the autumn of 1938; state house building ceased at the same time (Tooze 2007: 258).

Driven by geopolitical fantasies, Hitler's regime sought to overtake its adversaries by an accelerated rearmament programme so that it could launch a war before they caught up. The result was a series of increasingly risky ventures and crises in which successive new armament programmes were launched. Recent research has emphasised that the German economy was weak. Indeed, one of the perverted motives of the Nazi regime was to improve Germany's economic position by military conquest. But, despite some military success, the acquisition of armaments, railway rolling stock and gold reserves, the improvement in Germany's economic position was never as great as was expected. As late as 1944, 47 per cent of Germany's artillery was of foreign origin, mostly captured from the French, but, in economic terms, the conquests were not as productive as might have been hoped (Tooze 2007: 385). The difficulty was that the wealth of France and Belgium, for example, depended on foreign trade and once cut off from world markets they were impoverished (Mazower 2009: 260). Again Nazi Germany was always short of oil and sought by attempting to conquer the Caucasus to exploit the oil fields around Baku.

One consequence of the enormous demands made on the German economy during the war was the gradual collapse of the price system and a move to the physical control of resources. The inevitable result at the end of the war was the collapse of the currency. Thus by 1944 inflation was accelerating in Germany and the occupied territories. And at the same time Nazi bureaucrats were troubled that further pressure on resources would lead to a breakdown of the price system. A memorandum with the ominous title, 'Purchasing Power, Prices and War Finance', from a German planning agency concluded: 'The German economy is threatening to fall into anarchy, against which even an extended and improved system of economic controls will struggle in vain' (Tooze 2007: 642).

In an interview after the war with the war correspondent Henry Taylor, Herman Goering declared that experience during the war had confirmed that price controls were unworkable and urged America not to follow Germany's example (DiLorenzo 2005). It scarcely needs to be added that the Nazi regime used draconian measures to ensure compliance.

The British Inflation of the 1960s and 1970s

Much of post-war British economic history until 1980 was marked by accelerating inflation and increasing unemployment. The solution that gained support from politicians, economists and informed opinion was an 'incomes policy' to use the jargon of the time. The idea was that prices were the result of 'cost-push'. In other words, increases in wages were the cause of subsequent inflation. But this analysis is based on a simple mistake. Costs do not determine the prices of consumption goods; rather it is the value attributed to a consumption good that determines its price. In other words, the amount the consumer is prepared to pay for a particular good determines whether the producer can afford the resources of all kinds needed to produce the good in question.

Table 1   Britain's experiment with wage and price controls 1948–77

Period	Name/ description	Government	Voluntary/ compulsory	Institutions involves
Feb 48–Oct 50	Cripps–TUC	Labour	Voluntary	None
July 61–Mar 62	Selwyn Lloyd pay pause	Conservative	Voluntary	None
Apr 62–Oct 64	Guiding Light	Conservative	Voluntary	National Incomes Commission
Dec 64–July 66	Statement of Intent	Labour	Voluntary	National Board for Prices and Incomes (NBPI)
July 66–Dec 66	Freeze	Labour	Statutory	NPBI
Jan 67–June 67	Severe Restraint	Labour	Statutory	NPBI
June 67–Apr 68	Relaxation	Labour	Statutory	NBPI
Apr 68–June 70	Jenkins Renewed Restraint	Labour	Statutory	NPBI
Nov 70–Jan 73	Stage I Freeze	Conservative	Statutory	
Feb 73–Oct 73	Stage II Prices and Incomes Policy	Conservative	Statutory	Pay Board Price Commission
Nov 73–Feb 74	Stage III Prices and Incomes Policy	Conservative	Statutory	Pay Board Price Commission
Mar 74–June 74	Social Contract	Labour	Voluntary	
Aug 75–Jul 76	£6 pay rise limit	Labour	Compulsory (not statutory)	None
Aug 76–Jul 77	4.5% pay rise limit	Labour	Compulsory (not statutory	None

Source: Brittan and Lilley (1977: 154).

There was another more sophisticated rationalisation of incomes policies. It was argued that the role of incomes policy or 'wage restraint' was to prevent trade union power from increasing unemployment and hence reducing the need for stimulus to mitigate the unemployment caused. The idea that the government should legislate to reduce the wage-fixing, un-employment-causing trade union monopoly power was deemed politically impossible. The period, it will be remembered, was when Rab Butler's view that politics was the 'art of the possible' reigned. And politicians took a very cautious view of what was 'possible'.

In their study of British 'incomes policies' Samuel Brittan and Peter Lilley (Brittan and Lilley 1977) explain that, while Britain may have had limited economic success in the 1950s, 1960s and 1970s, it produced more different attempts to contain inflation by the control of incomes than any other country. Table 1 lists the 14 different incomes polices between 1948 and 1977.

As the table shows there was a succession of policies, commissions, agreements, hectoring, and moral suasion. Elderly connoisseurs of the period may remember 'The Guiding Light', the 'Three Wise Men', the 'Social Contract', the 'Pay Pause' and other compulsory or voluntary efforts to restrain wages.

But did the succession of incomes policies have any success? Figure 6 shows the steady rise of both inflation and unemployment and the failure of all wage and price ceilings. They prevented neither the rise in inflation nor a steady increase in unemployment.

Figure 6 UK unemployment and inflation 1949–80

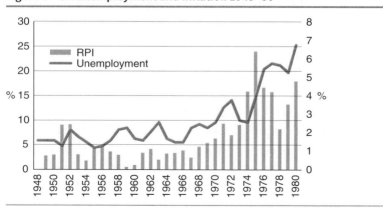

What unites these attempts to mitigate inflation with controls?

What do these four episodes of inflation, which provoked governments to attempt to mitigate the effects by wage and price controls, have in common? They cover nearly two millennia, spanning widely different times, political circumstances, civilisations and economic understanding. As we have seen, in the ancient world there was no understanding of economics as it is understood today. This had to wait until the Enlightenment and the development of economic theory in the 19th and 20th centuries. The Weimar and Nazi experiences with inflation can be seen as the direct effect of catastrophic loss of the tax base and in the Nazi response to imaginary strategic threats. The great Roman currency depreciation, which culminated in the Diocletian price controls, was the result of strategic threats that the Roman Empire did not have the resources to meet. Can the British multi-decade experience of accelerating inflation and income policies have the same explanation as the other historic inflations that we have reviewed above?

Despite the substantial differences, the Roman and Weimar experiences have very similar causes. Governments were seeking to acquire more resources than they could easily obtain through taxation. But this account appears not to explain the British inflation of the 1950s, 1960s and 1970s when there was no significant stress on British governments leading them to seek more resources from the economy than were available from taxation. The explanation here is a little different. It was believed that unemployment could be kept lower by a high level of aggregate demand. In other words, successive governments tried to keep unemployment low by artificial means – they tried to bring in to the economy more resources than was feasible, just as happened in the earlier periods in a somewhat different context. The British multi-decade experiment with wage and price controls was driven by mistaken economic theory. It was believed that, without burgeoning aggregate demand, high unemployment at an intolerable level would emerge. The result was as if Britain had lost a large proportion of its tax base or was under severe and immediate military threat requiring massive military spending. Unfortunately, workers soon began to bargain in terms of real rather than nominal wages and the ability of increased monetary demand to reduce unemployment even temporarily was steadily eroded. The British experience is different because the stress put upon the economy was self-imposed.

The key to explaining all these examples of currency depreciation or inflation is that governments maintain demand for resources that are greater than those that are, in fact, available to them. Sometimes the temptation to do this is very great and perhaps even the only practicable option is to inflate. But such circumstances will be very rare – the immediate prospect of invasion might be an example. Furthermore, price controls cannot be an effective way of dealing with the problems caused by rising prices.

Wage and price controls are ineffective

The most obvious conclusion from the analysis of these different experiences with inflation is that price controls and their little brother, wage controls or 'restraint', were unsuccessful. Despite the severest of threats, and it is hard to imagine anything more severe than treatment meted out by the Gestapo, there was no escape from inflation except by monetary continence. In each case, except for the British case, price and wage controls did not stop the abandonment of the currency and its replacement. As we saw, there was some evidence that price controls could for a time slow the pace of inflation but they could never bring it to an end. They also produced alarming and damaging side-effects, which are outlined below.

It is interesting to speculate on the cause and structure of the controls. If, as we have argued, inflation and currency depreciation is the result of excessive pressure by governments on available resources, then inflation is just a convenient tax that is cheap to impose. Its other advantage is that it is a tax that can be raised rapidly without interference from the legislature, if such exists. However, it is a crude tax, which is regressive: there are no tax exemptions for those on low incomes. It follows that one of the aims of price controls can be to mitigate the regressive character of the inflation tax. Thus price controls are usually focused on necessities such as food, rents and fuel. This can be seen in the disparate inflations of Rome and Weimar.

Price controls can also be seen as a reversion to a primitive face-to-face morality, which is inappropriate in the extended order of an abstract society. Thus Diocletian was wrong to ascribe the inflation of the 290s to the greed of merchants rather than the expansion of the money supply. But, as we have seen, without any concept of an economy and, consequently, without economic theory, it was very difficult for him to do otherwise.

Repressed inflation and price distortion

As we have seen, the most obvious effect of inflation is that it operates as a proportionate tax on all incomes, not just those of the better off. This prompts governments to seek to treat these symptoms with controls on the prices of necessities. One of the most damaging effects of sustained inflation is the need for re-pricing. Businessmen and consumers are forced continually to re-price their goods and services to adjust their business plans to each new monetary disturbance. Inflation forces participants to spend resources on price discovery and price adjustment which otherwise would be unnecessary, thus adding 'static' to the system, to use George Selgin's term (Selgin 1997: 33).

But the attempt by governments to suppress the effects of inflation is even more destructive. Prices play an important role in revealing where resources are needed most and least and in indicating to participants how to shift resources from one use to another. Price controls weaken this mechanism and hence result in inefficiencies, which are often extreme. One of the consequences is that price controls can produce shortages. Prices enforced at an unprofitable rate cause businessmen to withdraw goods from the market. In turn this leads to barter and transactions in the black market and the loss of the advantages of money.

Even if price controls are all-embracing and are aggressively enforced, prices cease to function and individuals are reduced to barter and governments turn to expropriation as they can acquire the resources in no other way. Thus both before and after Diocletian's experiment with price controls, the Roman administration expropriated resources and paid its soldiers in kind. Similarly, in the final years of the Nazi regime, physical controls of resources were used as the basis of the planning system.

One consequence of effective all-embracing price controls is that goods are withdrawn from the market and people have nothing on which to spend their money. Cash balances accumulate until the controls are removed when they are immediately exchanged for physical property. The result is that the currency in question immediately and dramatically falls in value and rapidly becomes useless.

Conclusion

Price and wage controls have been tried in a number of radically different economies and eras. The context has been currency depreciation or inflation and the consequences have been depressingly similar. Inflation may sometimes have been interrupted temporarily but it has never been eliminated or contained by such means. Inflation or currency depreciation tend to lead to price controls which are intended variously to mitigate some of the regressive character of the inflation tax and to contain inflation itself. Controls are often the result of a reversion to the 'ethics of small groups' where someone's economic gain is always seen as someone else's loss. Hence the discomfort of those ill-affected by inflation is supposed to be the result of the actions of merchants, property owners and others who gain. The obvious solution, it appears, is to restrain the actions of the merchants and property owners. But this approach is flawed as it is based on a mistaken understanding of the mechanism of inflation. Not surprisingly, the approach also fails, except for short periods, to mitigate inflation or its ill side effects.

References

Bresciani-Turroni, C. (1968) *The Economics of Inflation*. New York: Augustus M. Kelley.

Brittan, S. and Lilley, P. (1977) *The Delusion of Incomes Policy*. London: Maurice Temple Smith.

DiLorenzo, T. J. (2005). Four thousand years of price control. Mises Daily index, 10 November. http://mises.org/daily/1962/ (accessed 10 March 2015).

Finley, M. I. (1973) *The Ancient Economy*. London: Chatto & Windus.

Guttman, W. and Meehan, P. (1975) *The Great Inflation*. Farnborough: Saxon House.

Heath, P. (2006). Empire and development: the fall of the Roman west. http://www.historyandpolicy.org/policy-papers/papers/empire -and-development-the-fall-of-the-roman-west (accessed 10 March 2015).

Mazower, M. (2009) *Hitler's Empire*. London: Penguin.

Rostovtzeff, M. (1957) *The Social and Economic History of the Roman Empire*, Vol. 1. Oxford: Clarendon Press.

Selgin, G. (1997) *Less Than Zero*. London: Institute of Economic Affairs.

Tooze, A. (2007) *The Wages of Destruction*. London: Penguin.

Ward-Perkins, B. (2005) *The Fall of Rome*. Oxford University Press.

4 THE SIMPLE ECONOMICS OF WAGE FLOORS

W. S. Siebert

My daughter's ambition is to get a job in an office. She has Down's syndrome. She thinks that, if she works hard, someone, somewhere will give her a job. At £6.50 per hour, it's never going to happen. But at £2 per hour? Maybe.

Letter from Candice Baxter to
the *Daily Telegraph*, 17 October 2014

There is now no sizeable lobby in the UK campaigning for the abolition of the minimum wage.... In a poll of experts by the Institute for Government the minimum wage was voted the most successful UK government policy of the past 30 years, ahead of the Northern Ireland peace process.

Manning (2013: 65)

Introduction

A wage floor such as the minimum wage makes payment of low wages illegal. Such a floor clearly tends to reduce unskilled job opportunities, yet it is only one example of floors under working conditions placed by regulation. Other floors on terms and conditions of employment relate to requirements for protection against unfair dismissal, or discrimination and the provision of pensions through 'auto enrolment'. Moreover, we must remember that high welfare benefits also place a type of floor under wages, since for many it is not worth working for a wage lower than the welfare payments they could receive. The adverse effects of these floors can compound each other, particularly in a high tax environment, as we will show. High floors can also be imposed by union power, especially via extended collective agreements as in France.

The minimum wage from the beginning has been justified by the Low Pay Commission (2000: 18) as a means of achieving 'equity in the workplace'. But, in most private sector businesses, equity is already achieved, in the sense that wages approximate the revenue product of the marginal worker. Private sector competition drives this result though the public sector of course does not fit into this model so easily. If low wages are made illegal, then what happens is that the least productive workers cannot be employed. This result is demonstrated most clearly in the case of disabled workers, as shown in our opening quotation above. As Candice Baxter points out in her letter, her daughter could gain employment at £2 per hour, but certainly not at £6.50. One's heart goes out to her. The celebrations of the politicians in the Institute for Government, shown in our second quotation from Professor Manning, are premature.

Wage floors and other regulations of working conditions grow together with centralised government and are a part of the EU dirigiste tradition. The 1989 EU Charter on Fundamental Social Rights of Workers marks a watershed (see Addison and Siebert 1994), and has subsequently become the Social Chapter of the 1992 Treaty of Maastricht and the 1997 Treaty of Amsterdam. The Social Chapter sets floors to most aspects of employment conditions, including 'fair remuneration', working hours, freedom of association/unionisation, training, equal treatment for men and women (and others), compulsory worker consultative councils, and health and safety. In EU terms (Commission 2006: 5) 'the purpose of labour law is to offset the inherent economic and social inequality within the employment relationship'. In other words, decent wages and conditions are due to the efforts of politicians. Thus, the role of free markets and freedom of movement in defending the under-privileged is misunderstood.

Setting minimum wages is easy, but this deals with the symptoms of low pay and not the causes. The political payoff from minimum wage laws is immediate: the dispersion of wages is reduced and, since more women are low paid, so is the difference between male and female average pay (another mis-leading statistic). Yet nothing is done about the real problems in the labour market and the education system (see Kristian Niemietz 2012). The low level of skills acquired by children from our many single-parent families is ignored, as is the workless-ness among these families.[1] As for really disadvantaged groups such as the disabled, the minimum wage may do much harm. Opportunities may also be reduced for students who may be prevented from taking low-paid internships (and may have to volunteer instead), and for those whose main work is in the home but who would like to obtain some work to supplement household income or to obtain the benefits of socialising in the workplace. The best that can be said of the minimum wage policy is that it is irrelevant to real problems of inequality and worklessness. More likely, it is part of a package combined with other floors on working conditions which make matters worse – as exemplified by Greece.

This chapter begins by considering the research into the UK's national minimum wage, which is difficult given the lack of

---

1   26% of dependent children aged 0–18 live in single-parent families in the UK, which is almost twice as high as in France and Germany. The proportion of children being brought up in jobless families is consequently also high, around 20% (see OECD 2011a, Tables 1.1 and LMF1.1A), which reduces these children's education and em-ployment prospects.

regional variation and the confounding effects of high levels of welfare payments. Then we will look at the evidence from Canada and the US, where variation in the minimum across both countries gives a more suitable design for minimum wage evaluation. We will also discuss the interesting case of South Africa, where minimum wages were, for a time, used as a weapon in the struggle for white supremacy. We will also discuss results from OECD country panels, which arguably give the best design for minimum wage evaluation. Finally, we will extend the discussion to consider effects of minimum wages set by collective agreement: such minima are more detailed and intrusive, as shown by the study by Martins (2014) of the '30,000 minimum wages' set by collective agreements in Portugal.

UK evidence on employment effects

The UK is the worst place conceivable to test for minimum wage employment effects. Changes in the minimum have been quite small, they are country-wide (so there is no clear counterfactual), and they are carefully tailored to the unemployment situation so as not to exacerbate unemployment unduly (the economists on the Low Pay Commission are apolitical and well aware of negative employment effects). Compounding the problem is the changing welfare system, which also affects employment. We should remember that, in 1999, at the same time as the minimum wage was implemented, the government introduced Working Family Tax Credits, which were designed to encourage work and which would obviously tend to counteract minimum wage effects in the opposite direction. However, the UK research does need to be considered, if only to show that we need to be careful before concluding (see, for example, Leonard et al. 2014) from small measured UK minimum wage effects that conventional labour market models do not work.

The minimum wage and the welfare floor

The confounding effect of movements in welfare entitlements is shown in Figure 7. Here simple demand (D) and supply (S) curves

Figure 7   Welfare benefits confound minimum wage employment effects

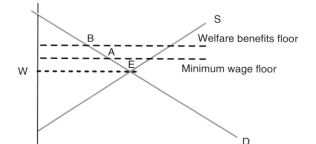

are drawn for the unskilled labour market. If a minimum wage is imposed, equilibrium moves from point E to point A. However, if welfare benefits are brought in, or raised above the minimum, then employment falls further, to point B. If welfare benefits are pre-existing, then the impact of the minimum wage on employment will be muted. The diagram is a simplification, because apprentices and trainees will continue working for less than welfare benefits, as we discuss later. Also, welfare benefits – certainly in the UK[2] – may vary with income from employment so that people receive some benefits even if they are earning a wage below the welfare floor. But the tendency remains – there is an interaction between the welfare system and the effects of minimum wages. Moreover,

---

2   The Working Tax Credit is effectively a job subsidy and is conditional upon work, though the much bigger Child Tax Credit provides an effective welfare floor.

Table 2   Net benefit replacement rates as a per cent of income from work over 60 months unemployment

	France		Germany		US		UK	
	no children	two children	no children	two children	no children	two children	no children	two children
2001	60.3	70.3	59.6	73.5	15.2	43.0	55.0	64.9
2012	53.6	63.2	49.9	70.4	24.8	42.8	51.0	72.4
Change 2012– 2001	−6.7	−7.1	−9.7	−3.0	9.6	−0.2	−4.0	7.5

Source: OECD Benefits and Wages Statistics. http://www.oecd.org/els/benefitsandwagesstatistics. htm (accessed 10 March 2015).

Notes: Replacement rates are calculated based on incomes after any tax and social security contributions have been deducted, and any cash benefits received. It is assumed that the family qualifies for cash housing assistance and social assistance 'top ups'. The figures give unweighted averages relative to full-time earnings levels of 67 per cent and 100 per cent of mean worker earnings.

if welfare benefits are reduced or reformed in other ways, employment will increase, confusing minimum wage effects.

Table 2 shows welfare trends, including the housing assistance component. Unfortunately, this series on net replacement rates is not available prior to 2001; however, we can analyse most of the period since the introduction of the minimum wage. As can be seen, replacement rates have declined in France and Germany (the Hartz reforms), increased for single people in the US, and increased for families but not for single people in the UK. In fact, the UK's family replacement rates are now among the most generous in the OECD (Niemietz 2012: 46). However, some of the welfare is contingent on working at least 16 hours, and so encourages some work. In fact, Gregg et al. (2012: 22) estimate that employment of single women rose by 4 per cent when tax credits were introduced: this worked against minimum wage effects on employment.

Payment below the minimum

Figure 8 demonstrates two important points about the progress of wages after the minimum was introduced. We see that a

Figure 8   Effects of the minimum wage on earnings: 1998 and 1999
compared

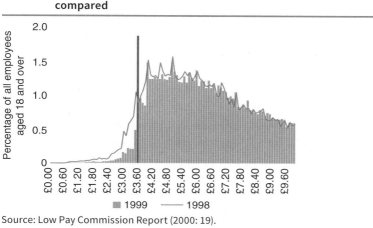

Source: Low Pay Commission Report (2000: 19).

substantial number of people were freely working for low wages
in 1998 prior to the implementation of the minimum. About 6
per cent of the workforce is in that lower tail which grades slowly
down to zero, reflecting the alternatives and productivity levels
of the individuals concerned. Here Mrs Baxter's daughter would
have found her job.

Secondly, we see that, even after the minimum was introduced,
many wish to be paid below it. Low pay is a continuing phenomenon, with currently about 200,000 adults (21 and over, i.e. 1 per cent
of the adult workforce) paid below the minimum (LPC 2014: 133).
In fact, the real total is probably double this figure (Kay 2010: 35)
when we add the large number of under 21s. Much of this non-com-
pliance occurs with apprentices, who are quite happy to receive
low wages while training, as do students in general. In fact, about
70 per cent of 18–20-year-old hairdressing apprentices (LPC 2014:
134) currently refuse to accept the minimum wage, for which of
course the Low Pay Commission and trade unions wrongly blame
the employer. A further group comprises unpaid interns and vol-
unteers, who do not enter wage distributions like Figure 7 at all,

but whom the Commission sees as unfairly avoiding its system. The important point is that many people see it worthwhile to work for low or no wages. This is particularly so for students and people training in order to raise their future wages.[3]

Adverse employment effects

A good study of adverse employment effects is provided by Dickens et al. (2012), who focus on part-time women where coverage by the minimum is about 10 per cent, twice as high as for full-timers (LPC 2014, Fig. 2.1). They establish a counterfactual by comparing part-timers whose wages are raised by the minimum to those paid just above that level (10 per cent above). This comparison group will have similar skills and welfare benefit options. They find that the introduction of the minimum in 1999 caused the year-on-year probability of part-time women retaining a job to fall from around 0.70 to 0.65. Another way of putting this finding is that before the minimum wage, median job duration was about 1.9 years for part-time women earning around the minimum, falling to 1.7 years after the minimum wage, that is, a fall of around 10 per cent. They do not find employment effects caused by the up-ratings since 1999 as they have been too small to have much effect. For example, the recent up-rating from £6.31 to £6.50 gives a maximum uplift of 1.5 per cent to about 5 per cent of the workforce. As well as being small relative to welfare benefit changes, minimum wage increases have been lower in times of recession. Overall, this means that it is difficult to detect effects of changes in the minimum wage, but this result does not mean that higher increases in the future will be harmless.

---

3   See Gorry (2013: 72) for a good paper on how the minimum wage obstructs training: 'Inexperienced workers are unable to pay for their training through reductions in their wages. To gain experience, they must maintain employment in a segment of the labour market characterized by high job separation rates' – their probability of unemployment consequently rises.

While minimum wage increases so far have been small, a further piece of research by Riley (2013) brings out the negative effects of the altogether larger change that the introduction of a minimum wage equal to the 'living wage' could have (see also Siebert 2014). Currently, the 'living wage' is calculated to be £7.65 outside London, and £8.80 in London (Living Wage 'Commission' 2014). Such a change would mean wage increases for about 25 per cent of the workforce, and raise labour costs of young unskilled (non-university) workers by as much as 14 per cent in sectors such as hotels and catering and retailing. Riley shows not only that the demand elasticity for labour is negative, but also that cross-price elasticities are generally positive, precisely in accordance with conventional economic theory. In other words, when the wage of young inexperienced and unskilled people rises, their employment falls and the employment of substitutes such as educated workers and older workers increases. Thus, 300,000 young unskilled workers would lose their jobs, but some skilled and older workers would gain employment, with the overall loss of jobs reduced to 160,000. Increasing the minimum wage to the living wage would therefore enable older, better educated workers to gain at the expense of unskilled youth, as happens in France, but of course with serious long-term consequences for those trapped outside the labour market.

Britain's unskilled youth

The current dark situation for Britain's unskilled youth is shown in Tables 3 and 4, covering the period since the minimum wage began. Table 3 shows that labour force participation has declined for all the disadvantaged groups except the disabled (whose participation remains low). Admittedly, it appears that our youth participation rate is better than that in France. However, the UK lags France on another measure, which is shown in Table 4, the percentage of 15–19-year-olds in the NEET (not in education,

Table 3   Adverse changes in employment for unskilled workers: labour force participation rate (% of the population in each group)

	All working age	No qualifications	Disabled people	18–20 years old	16–24 years old	France 15–24
2000	71.7	50.8	37.7	61.2	69.7	35.6
2013	71.6	42.6	42.1	47.0	61.7	37.6
Change 2000–2013	–0.1	–8.2	4.4	–14.2	–8.0	2.0

Sources: Commission (2014, Table 2.11) and OECD Employment Outlook (2014).

Table 4   NEETs – country trends (% of 15–19-year-olds not in education, employment or training)

	France	Germany	Italy	US	UK	OECD average
1997	2.9	5.0	15.2	7.1	8.0	9.2
2012	6.9	3.0	12.0	7.7	9.5	7.6
Change 2012–1997	4.0	–2.0	–3.2	0.6	1.5	–1.6

Sources: OECD Education at a Glance (2014, Chart C5.3), and OECD Doing Better for Families (2011a, Figure 1.15).

employment and training) group. Here we see that the UK's percentage has been growing and at 9.5 per cent is the worst of the five major economies shown, and worse than the OECD average. In summary, Tables 3 and 4 show that the inequality of life chances has been growing, despite the Low Pay Commission's mission to reduce 'inequity in the workplace'.

People who reject the orthodox explanation for the small UK minimum wage effects need an alternative. They bring forward the ideas of single buyer power (i.e. 'monopsony': see Manning 2013) or of 'efficiency wages' (Leonard et al. 2014) to explain the perceived market failure. Ironically, these two theories have diametrically opposed views of what happens in free markets. The monopsony theory implies that wages are too low: firms operate with unfilled vacancies, because raising wages enough to eliminate the backlog would require pay increases for all. But

Table 5   Firm size and employment, UK 2009

Number – Private Sector, 2009 (including public corporations and nationalised bodies)			
		Enterprises (thousands)	Employees (millions)
Enterprises without employees		3,620	0
Enterprises with employees		1,220	18.2
Enterprise sizes:	1–4	795	1.8
	5–49	390	4.6
	50–249	30	2.6
	250–499	3	1.0
	500 or more	3	8.1
Central and local government		5	5.4
Non-profit		84	1.9

Source: BIS, Enterprise Directorate (2010). https://www.gov.uk/government/organisations/
department-for-business-innovation-skills/about/statistics (accessed 10 March 2015).
Notes: An enterprise is the smallest group of legal units which has autonomy. It is based on the Inter-departmental Business Register (IDBR) formed from VAT or PAYE records collected by HMRC. Since the VAT threshold (£67,000 in 2009) excludes small firms, estimates of their numbers are then added using Labour Force Survey figures of the numbers of self-employed (4.1m). Private households and temping agencies are excluded.
There is no lower bound for inclusion as an enterprise, hence the smallest amount of enterprise activity counts – hence there are many 'no employee' enterprises which have only working proprietors in the business. 'Employees' have a contract of employment, and include part-timers. Working proprietors are self-employed (but working directors of companies are counted as employees).

the efficiency wage theory implies that wages are, in a sense, 'too high': wages are above the market-clearing rate because paying well is a cheap way to help supervisors generate extra employee effort.

In fact neither theory fits well with the UK firm size structure, which is shown in Table 5. We see that the UK has 3.6 million enterprises which only employ the owner, and obviously have no monopsony power or difficulty with supervision. There are also 1.2 million enterprises which employ workers, but the vast majority of these (97 per cent) employ fewer than 50 workers, and again can have no monopsony power or supervision issues. In fact, it is only the 6,000 firms that employ more than 250 to which these theories might apply. However, these firms tend to pay higher wages in any case and so the minimum wage is broadly irrelevant for them. It is much more likely that unskilled and inexperienced workers lose from the minimum, and indeed their unemployment rises more than proportionately as the minimum rises, as shown in Gorry's (2013) elegant model. Monopsony and efficiency wage theories would seem irrelevant.

International evidence on the minimum wage

It is fair to say that the UK evidence on the minimum wage does not find large employment effects. It does find some disturbing trends. However, the background to the UK's minimum wage ensures that any statistical analysis is likely to lead to inconclusive results. For a more thorough analysis, we need to look at countries where there is variation of the minimum either for regions within a country (as in Canada or the US) or we need to look at the variation provided by cross-country panels. A country with low welfare payments (for example, the US) is also easier to analyse. Let us first consider Canadian and US results, and then examine South Africa, which starkly underlines how minimum wages can be misused by skilled workers to cut out unskilled competition.[4]

Canada

Canada provides some of the best conditions for research into the effects of minimum wages since the ten Canadian provinces have

---

4   Another interesting country to consider could be France with its exceptionally high minimum (Gorry 2013). But France presents the same problems as the UK: lack of within-country variation, plus the confounders of high welfare payments and high taxes. China is also a possibility, with good variation provided by different minimum wages in different cities. Fang and Lin (2013) provide evidence of strong negative minimum wage effects using city data, which are better than the province data used by Wang and Gunderson (2012), who find inconclusive effects at least for Eastern China. However, it is too early to draw conclusions from China, since it is so large and heterogeneous with complications to the analysis caused by migrant labour and a large state-owned sector.

different minimum wage policies, sometimes with considerable bite. Good time series data are also available. A convincing body of Canadian literature has thus built up, starting with Baker et al.'s (1999) study of nine provinces from 1975 to 1993. This study finds that a 10 per cent increase in the minimum wage reduces teenage employment by 2.5 per cent and that it takes six years for the full effect to be revealed. Canadian data are also used in the recent study for 1997–2008 by Campolieti et al. (2014: 587), who find a short-run elasticity of −0.16 for the 15–24-year-old group. Importantly, they note that their method cannot capture long-run minimum wage effects (since they follow individuals for only six months); they recommend doubling this elasticity to derive the full picture in the long run. That would lead to a long-run elasticity of demand for labour of about −0.3, leading a 10 per cent increase in the minimum wage to increase unemployment by about 3 per cent of the workforce among the affected group. A similar finding for teen employment is made by Sen et al. (2011). Interestingly, older workers' employment appears to increase with minimum wage increases (Fang and Gunderson 2009), suggesting they are substituted for less productive youths, as we have already seen for the UK. The minimum's adverse effect using good data thus becomes clearer.

A possible reason for the clarity of the Canadian effect is that Canada's minimum wage workers tend more to be in the tradeable goods exporting sectors. In this situation, the higher minimum wage undermines competitiveness and causes employment reduction. The position is different if minimum wage workers are concentrated in non-tradeable activities such as retailing or construction (as in the UK). In this case, a rise in the minimum wage simply 'takes wages out of competition' and this result can even be advantageous, especially for large firms (see Cox and Oaxaca (1982) and, more recently, Neumark and Wascher (2008)). Costs go up, but the increase is faced by everyone, and prices can increase to offset this given the absence of overseas competition. This factor might account for the weaker disemployment results found in the US studies of the restaurant sector noted below (e.g. Addison et al. 2012). Magruder's (2013) study of minimum wages in Indonesia emphasises the importance of whether the sectors mainly affected are in the tradeable or non-tradeable sectors.

The United States

Turning to research on the US, there is now much technical controversy raised by the work of Allegretto et al. (2011) and Dube et al. (2010), well summarised in the recent work by Neumark et al. (2014). The key problem is how to specify control groups when policy changes. Still, Neumark et al.'s exhaustive analysis (2014: 627) concludes that, when the time trends are correctly specified, the elasticity of teen employment to the minimum wage remains in or near the −0.1 to −0.2 range. In other words, an increase in the minimum of 10 per cent would reduce employment by 1–2 per cent. Elasticity of employment in the restaurant sector is lower, but still negative and significant at around −0.05 or −0.06 (2014: 644). Thus the adverse effect remains.

We cannot leave US minimum wage research without mentioning the famous but weak Card and Krueger (1995) studies of the response of fast-food restaurant employment to increases in minimum wages. The best-known of these studies is the contrast of New Jersey with Pennsylvania, the latter having no increase in its minimum wage. This research is the basis for stating that the conventional economic view that minimum wages cause unemployment is a 'myth'. But the New Jersey versus Pennsylvania study is only based on four data points. The fact that there are many restaurants in the four samples (New Jersey before and after, and the control, Pennsylvania, before and after) does not help increase the power of the test since the same minimum wage regime applies in each. It is also worth noting again that the restaurant sector is always likely to suffer less from a minimum wage because it is sheltered from international competition. The work is sold as 'a powerful new challenge to the conventional view', but this is misleading – it is a very specific challenge and a weak one at that.

South Africa

The evidence from South Africa shows what happens when minimum wages really go wrong. South Africa under white control, before 1994, had what it described as a 'civilised labour policy' aiming to favour white employment (Van der Horst 1942: 250; also Siebert 1986). A pillar of this policy was high minimum wages and extended collective agreements, which meant that only white workers, who were generally better educated than non-whites, could gain employment. Minimum wages were thus used as a weapon against the majority. The higher costs that resulted were not so much of a problem when it came to employment because tariff barriers prevented imports competing with domestic businesses. (However, the minimum combined with the trade regulation raised costs to consumers – including poor consumers.) The high minimum wage system continues to this day, with extended collective agreements in particular supporting a strongly unionised African labour elite (Schultz 1998). For example, a union worker in manufacturing receives 70 per cent more than a non-union worker (Schultz 1998: 700). The system has since been extended to agriculture and domestic service. In agriculture the increase in pay has been large at 17 per cent (Bhorat et al. 2012), and employment has contracted considerably, by 14 per cent. In domestic service, again protected from international competition, the effects might not have been so bad (Dinkelman 2012; Hertz 2005), but only 25 per cent of households appear to comply. Thus, we see a policy originally designed to hurt African workers is now being carried forward by African politicians and unions themselves, and still hurting African workers.

International studies

Finally, we will consider the evidence from international cross-country panels. This research design gives the most variation in minimum wages and thus helps create more robust studies. Negative employment effects from minimum wages are clear in all the studies. Admittedly there are some difficulties of comparability. In particular, countries such as Germany, Italy, Denmark and Sweden have no national minimum wage as such, but use legally enforceable extended collective agreements. Still, such agreements are effective minima (see below). There is also the difficulty of allowing for widely different welfare regimes, and these studies typically use the OECD's index of gross benefit replacement rates, which leaves out housing benefit, which is important in the UK.[5] However, it is hoped that the gross replacement rates capture the trends, and in any case the studies all control for country and time fixed effects.

Neumark and Wascher (2004) provide the first comprehensive treatment, analysing 17 OECD countries over the period 1975–2000. Their main finding (2004: 243) is that the minimum wage elasticity of teenage (15–19) employment is significantly negative, in the −0.2 to −0.4 range. In other words, the implication is that an increase of 10 per cent in the minimum would cause a 2–4 per cent fall in employment in the affected group. More recently, there have been OECD-based international studies by Dolton and Bondibene (2012) of youth employment, and Addison and Ozturk (2012) of female employment. Dolton and Bondibene (2012) also find a large negative effect of minimum wages on youth employment, with an elasticity of −0.3 to −0.4, most of this result coming in recession as might be expected. Addison and Ozturk (2012, Table 4) find a negative effect for the adult female

---

5   Hence in Addison and Ozturk (2012, Table 2b) the replacement rate for the UK averages only 20 per cent, much lower than the actual 60 per cent shown in Table 2.

employment-to-population rate, with an elasticity of −0.14 in the short run, and more in the long run when lagged effects are taken into account. Interestingly, there is an indication in this study (2012, Table 7) that the elasticity is larger (−0.34) in countries and time periods when employment protection law (EPL) is strict, as we would expect (see below). Thus, there is an unambiguous picture of strong negative minimum wage effects on lower-productivity groups in the international panel-based literature, which provides arguably the best foundation for research.

Collectively set minimum wages

Collectively set minimum wages arise when a collective agreement is extended by law to third parties within an industry or sector. A detailed set of minimum wages (and conditions) covering many job types and levels is thereby established for the industry or sector. Martins (2014) shows how the process works in the case of Portugal. Such extensions are the result of so-called 'erga omnes' (towards others) regulations, and have the aim of reducing non-union, low-wage competition. They are common (see Murtin et al. 2014) in countries where the unions are politically powerful – for example, are part funded or privileged by the state as in Greece or France or South Africa – but where local union power is low (again, France and Greece).[6] In these circumstances, unions have the power to bring about these regulations and also need to do so if they are to exercise their monopoly powers, since non-union firms are so prevalent. The picture is given in Table 6, where we see that France, Spain, Germany and Italy all have high use of extension arrangements. The important point is that erga

---

6   The UK used to have an erga omnes arrangement for unions to petition for exten-sion of their agreements, but Thatcher dismantled it (see Addison and Siebert 2000) with the 1980 Employment Act. The 'fair wages resolution' requiring government contractors to observe terms no less favourable than those obtaining under collec-tive agreements was also dropped at this time.

omnes regulations enable the setting of detailed minimum wage floors, floors that are determined by big business and labour in the capital cities – Athens, Rome, Paris – with little concern for conditions in the provinces. Hence, a net of various minimum wages is thrown over the country.

Research on this type of minimum wage setting builds on the literature of union power raising unemployment, which of course has long been controversial because a number of factors that influence unemployment can be correlated. Recent work is reported in the OECD's (2011b: 152) study of inequality using the OECD panel of countries over 1984–2007. Here there is shown to be a well-determined negative effect of collective bargaining coverage on employment rates. High tax rates and employment protection legislation hurt too. The most recent work using the OECD panel is by Murtin et al. (2014) with a more extensive

Table 6   Collectively set minimum wages, early 2000s

	Canada	Denmark	France	Germany	Greece	Italy	Norway
Coverage extension	4	0	79	48	30	46	15
Use of erga omnes clauses	No	No	High	High	High	High	Some
Union density	31	75	9	28	30	34	56
Government revenue % GDP	40	55	50	45	38	47	57

	Portugal	South Africa	Spain	Sweden	UK	US
Coverage extension	49	10	57	1	9	4
Use of erga omnes clauses	High	Some	High	No	No	No
Union density	25	25	15	81	34	14
Government revenue % GDP	40	27	36	54	40	31

Sources: Murtins et al. (2014), Industriall Global Union (2014). http://www.industriall-europe.eu/committees/CB/2014/Increasing%20cover%20rate-EN.pdf (accessed 10 March 2015).; Visser (2013), Godfrey (2007), OECD Government at a Glance (2013, Table 3.11).
Notes: Coverage extension measured as collective agreement coverage minus percentage unionisation.

Figure 9 High taxes magnify the minimum wage disemployment effect

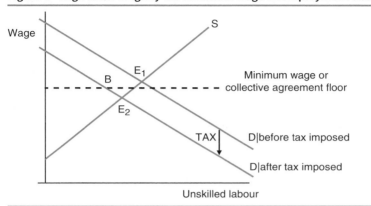

Unskilled labour

model, this time of unemployment. Their main innovation is to use collective agreement coverage extension, as shown in Table 6, which they find interacts with taxes (also shown in Table 6 as government revenue) to raise unemployment. Their minimum wage variable also raises unemployment, again more so when taxes are high.

These interaction results can be explained with the aid of Figure 9. Again we have the conventional demand (D) and supply (S) curves for unskilled labour, and start with a no-tax equilibrium at E_1. Now, assume a tax is imposed, so that the net demand curve for labour shifts inwards to D|net tax as shown. Without the minimum wage or collective agreement floor, the new equilibrium would be at E_2 with a lower wage, and less employment (but no disequilibrium unemployment). However, if there is a wage floor, the wage cannot fall so much, and the employment fall to B is greater. At B there is also disequilibrium unemployment. Therefore, according to this simple model, a rise in tax sweeps more into the minimum wage and extended collective agreement net, causing more unemployment; the empirical results support this theoretical observation.

There are also instructive results from two country case studies of Portugal and Greece involving extended agreements. As can be seen from Table 6, both of these countries have used such agreements extensively, though they are now restricted by recent debt bailout agreements.[7] Martins's (2014) analysis of Portugal over 2007–11 links unemployment to extensions of agreements to non-parties, and shows that average employment levels in affected sectors drop by 2 per cent in the four months following extensions, as firms stop hiring and close down. Since the wage increase is 2–4 per cent, the implied elasticity is between –0.5 and –1 (Martins 2014: 14). Peripheral employment of temporary workers and subcontractors meanwhile increases, as we would expect. This temporary worker result is the same as that for the Greek study (Anagnostopoulos and Siebert 2015), based on a survey of 200 provincial firms, which finds that low-paying firms near the minimum are more likely to employ temporary workers. The Greek study also shows that these effects persist even though many Greek firms do not in fact pay the minimum – they remain small so as to avoid the attention of the labour inspectorate. The minimum wage and extended collective agreements coupled with high taxes thus not only reduce employment, but push firms to be too small.[8]

---

7   In Greece, for example (see Commission (2014: 49) and LABREF database), the government in 2011 and 2012 agreed to reduce minimum pay rates by 22 per cent (32 per cent for young people). It also agreed to suspend extension of occupational and sector collective agreements, and to allow firm-level agreements which could be less favourable than the sector-level agreement. According to IndustriALL (2014), measures such as this caused Greek sector agreements to fall from 65 to 14 in 2013, and in Portugal (Martins 2014), coverage fell from 1.8 million in 2008 to 290,000 in 2012.

8   Thus in Greece and Portugal firms are too small, with over 95% employing fewer than 10 people, compared with an OECD average of about 85% (see OECD 2011c). Alternatively, if policing of the extended agreements is effective, as in South Africa, small firms can be prevented from growing enough (see Magruder 2012). The point is, regulation breeds regulation.

Conclusions and thoughts on real help for the unskilled

Minimum wages do have adverse employment effects broadly in line with conventional economic models. UK studies generally find small effects, but the UK environment is poorly suited to measure such effects given the changes in welfare benefits and the lack of regional variation. Matters become clearer when we turn to more suitable empirical settings, which provide clear evidence of an adverse effect of minimum wages on employment.

Better ways to help the poor would involve raising skills or, in the shorter term before such policies took meaningful effect, the provision of some kind of employment subsidy through the welfare system. When it comes to raising skills, the family is crucial, as is education. Encouragement of stable families and better, less unionised and more competitive school systems is difficult, but they are important policy priorities. High welfare simply makes these problems worse in the long term, as well described by Charles Murray (1984, 2012).

A quick and well-targeted way of helping the working poor is by subsidising low-paid work, a policy which contradicts the minimum wage. People have their earnings topped up by the taxpayer, and are therefore prepared to work for less, which expands their job opportunities. In fact, such a policy has been in place in the UK ever since 1999 when the Working Families Tax Credit was introduced (Azmat 2006), modelled on the US Earned Income Tax Credit (Hotz and Scholtz 2000), and since expanded with Working Tax Credit. Reforms to the system would be desirable, but the idea of not removing benefits entirely when people work in low-paid jobs is an important one. Tax credits conditional on work currently encourage about 2.5 million workers into work (see Browne and Hood 2012), but they only account for about 5 per cent of the amount paid out to working-age welfare recipients, and are dwarfed in particular by child tax credits and housing benefits. Reform of this whole system is needed (see Bourne and Shackleton 2014).

In conclusion, there is no need for analysts (e.g. Holmlund 2014; Schmitt 2013) to worry about 'discernible effects' of minimum wages on employment. The effects are discernible, when properly measured. Hence it is indeed probable that the UK's dismal youth labour market performance since 1999 is partly attributable to the imposition of the minimum wage interacting with high tax rates. This is also the case with the poorly functioning youth labour markets of Portugal and Greece, and others such as France and South Africa. Moreover, the way in which more skilled workers displace the less skilled, and temporary workers displace permanent workers is in line with conventional economic models. Obviously, in a political world which denies productivity differences – including skills, gender, age and disability differences[9] – the differential effects of minimum wages are politically unwelcome This is all the more reason for economists to stick to their guns and look for real, not fake, ways to help the poor.

Acknowledgments

I would like to thank John Addison for valuable comments, and also participants in Birmingham University's BSc Business Management debates in labour economics. The usual disclaimers apply.

---

9   The disability pressure groups often do the disabled no favours. For example (LPC 2005: 124), Mothercare for Children in Hospital Ltd (MCCH) is politically correct: 'the minimum wage is a positive step to reducing stigma, discrimination and workplace exploitation ... it has acted as a catalyst to change', etc. But Shaw Employment Services is blunt: 'Both client and provider are finding that instead of being more able to help the disabled achieve employment, the Government, through the NMW, has inadvertently created the first barrier' (LPC 2003: 105).

References

Addison, J., Blackburn, M. and Cotti, C. (2012) Labour market outcomes: county-level estimates from the restaurant-and-bar sector. *British Journal of Industrial Relations* 50: 412–35.

Addison, J. and Ozturk, O. (2012) Minimum wages, labor market institutions, and female employment: a cross-country analysis. *Industrial and Labor Relations Review* 65: 779–809.

Addison, J. and Siebert, W. S. (1994) Recent developments in social policy in the new European Union. *Industrial and Labor Relations Review* 48: 5–27.

Addison, J. and Siebert, W. S. (2000) Labor market reform in the UK: from Thatcher to Blair. *Journal of Private Enterprise* 15: 1–34.

Allegretto, S., Dube, A. and Reich, M. (2011) Do minimum wages really reduce teen employment? Accounting for heterogeneity and selectivity in state panel data. *Industrial Relations* 50: 205–40.

Anagnostopoulos, A. and Siebert, W. S. (2015) The impact of Greek labour market regulation on temporary and family employment – evidence from a new survey. *International Journal of Human Resource Management* (forthcoming). http://dx.doi.org/10.1080/09585192.201 5.1011190 (accessed 10 March 2015).

Azmat, G. (2006) The incidence of an earned income tax credit: evaluating the impact on wages in the UK. London School of Economics, CEP Discussion Paper 724.

Baker, M., Benjamin, D. and Stanger, S. (1999) The highs and lows of the minimum wage effect: a time-series cross-section study of the Canadian law. *Journal of Labor Economics* 17: 18–50.

Bhorat, H., Kanbur, R. and Stanwix, B. (2013) Estimating the impact of minimum wages on employment, wages and nonwage benefits: the case of agriculture in South Africa. Cornell University, School of Applied Economics and Management, WP 2013-05.

Bourne, R. and Shackleton, J. R. (2014) The minimum wage: silver bullet or poisoned chalice? Institute of Economic Affairs Briefing 14.01.

Brown, J. and Hood, A. (2012) A survey of the UK benefit system. IFS Briefing Note BN13. London: Institute for Fiscal Studies.

Campolieti, M., Gunderson, M. and Lee, B. (2014) Minimum wage effects on permanent versus temporary minimum wage employment. *Contemporary Economic Policy* 32: 578–91.

Card, D. and Krueger, A. (1995) *Myth and Measurement: The New Economics of the Minimum Wage*. Princeton University Press.

Commission (2006) Green Paper – Modernising labour law to meet the challenges of the 21st century. Brussels 22.11.2006 COM(2006) 708 final.

Commission (2014) The Second Economic Adjustment Programme for Greece. Occasional Papers 192, April. Brussels: Directorate-General for Economic and Financial Affairs.

Corak, M. (2013) Income inequality, equality of opportunity, and intergenerational mobility. *Journal of Economic Perspectives* 27: 79–102.

Cox, J. and Oaxaca, R. (1982) The political economy of minimum wage legislation. *Economic Inquiry* 20: 533–50.

Dickens, R., Riley, R. and Wilkinson, D. (2012) Re-examining the impact of the national minimum wage on earnings, employment and hours: the importance of recession and firm size. University of Sussex and National Institute of Economic and Social Research. http://www.sheffield.ac.uk/polopoly_fs/1.247213!/file/E1_riley.pdf (accessed 10 March 2015).

Dinkelman, T. and Ranchod, V. (2012) Evidence on the impact of minimum wage laws in an informal sector: domestic workers in South Africa. *Journal of Development Economics* 99: 27–45.

Dolton, P. and Bondibene, C. (2012) The international experience of minimum wages in an economic downturn. *Economic Policy* 27: 99–142.

Dube, A., Lester, T. and Reich, M. (2010), Minimum wage effects across state borders: estimates using contiguous counties. *Review of Economics and Statistics* 92: 945–64.

Fang, T. and Gunderson, M. (2009) Minimum wage impacts on older workers: longitudinal estimates from Canada. *British Journal of Industrial Relations* 47: 371–87.

Fang, T. and Lin, C. (2013) Minimum wages and employment in China. IZA Discussion Paper 7813.

Godfrey, S., Theron, J. and Visser, M. (2007) The state of collective bargaining in South Africa. UCT: Development Policy Research Unit Research Paper 07/130.

Gorry, A. (2013) Minimum wages and youth unemployment. *European Economic Review* 64: 57–75.

Gregg, P., Hurrell, A. and Whittaker, M. (2012) *Creditworthy – Assessing the Impact of Tax Credits*. London: Resolution Foundation.

Hertz, T. (2005) The effect of minimum wages on the employment and earnings of South Africa's domestic service workers. Upjohn Institute Working Paper 05-120.

Holmlund, B. (2014) What do labor market institutions do? *Labour Economics* 30: 62–69.

Hotz, V. and Scholtz, J. (2000) Not perfect, but still pretty good: the EITC and other policies to support the US low-wage labour market. OECD Economic Studies 31.

IndustriALL (2014) Negotiating our future! Collective Bargaining and Social Policy Conference, Vienna. http://www.industriall-eur ope.eu/committees/CB/2014/Increasing%20cover%20rate-EN.pdf (accessed 10 March 2015).

Kay, L. (2010) *Escaping the Poverty Trap*. London: Policy Exchange.

Leonard, M., Stanley, T. and Doucouliagos, H. (2014) Does the UK minimum wage reduce employment? A meta-regression analysis. *British Journal of Industrial Relations* 52: 499–520.

Living Wage Commission (2014) *Work That Pays*. London: Joseph Rowntree Trust.

LPC (2000) *The National Minimum Wage: The Story So Far*. Second Report of the Low Pay Commission. London: Low Pay Commission.

LPC (2001) *The National Minimum Wage – Making a Difference*, Vol. 1, Cm 5075. London: Low Pay Commission.

LPC (2003) *Low Pay Commission Report 2003 – Building on Success*, London: Low Pay Commission.

LPC (2005) *Low Pay Commission Report 2005*, Cm 6475. London: Low Pay Commission.

LPC (2014) *Low Pay Commission Report 2014*, Cm 8816. London: Low Pay Commission.

Magruder, J. (2012) High unemployment yet few small firms: the role of centralized bargaining in South Africa. *American Economic Journal: Applied Economics* 4: 138–66.

Magruder, J. (2013) Can minimum wages cause a big push? Evidence from Indonesia. *Journal of Development Economics* 100: 48–62.

Manning, A. (2013) Minimum wages: a view from the UK. *Perspektiven der Wirtschaftspolitik* 14: 57–66.

Martins, P. (2014) 30,000 minimum wages: the economic effects of collective bargaining extensions. IZA Discussion Paper 8540.

Murray, C. (1984) *Losing Ground: American Social Policy 1950–1980*. New York: Basic Books.

Murray, C. (2012) *Coming Apart: The State of White America 1960–2010*. New York: Crown Forum.

Murtin, F., de Serres, A. and Hijzen, A. (2014) Unemployment and the coverage extension of collective wage agreements. *European Economic Review* 71: 52–66.

Neumark, D. and Wascher, W. (2004) Minimum wages, labor market institutions and youth unemployment: a cross-national analysis. *Industrial and Labor Relations Review* 57: 223–48.

Neumark, D. and Wascher, W. (2008) Minimum wages and low-wage workers: how well does reality match the rhetoric? *Minnesota Law Review* 92: 1296–316.

Neumark, D., Salas, J. and Wascher, W. (2014) Revisiting the minimum wage-employment debate: throwing out the baby with the bathwater? *Industrial and Labor Relations Review* 67 (supplement): 608–48.

Niemietz, K. (2012) *Redefining the Poverty Debate*. London: Institute of Economic Affairs.

OECD (2011a) *Doing Better for Families*. Paris: OECD Publishing. http://dx.doi.org/10.1787/9789264098732-en (accessed 10 March 2015).

OECD (2011b) *Divided We Stand: Why Inequality Keeps Rising*. Paris: OECD Publishing. http://dx.doi.org/10.1787/9789264119536-en (accessed 10 March 2015).

OECD (2011c) *Entrepreneurship at a Glance 2011*. Paris: OECD Publishing. http://dx.doi.org/10.1787/9789264097711-en (accessed 10 March 2015).

OECD (2014) *Education at a Glance 2014: OECD Indicators*. OECD Publishing. http://dx.doi.org/10.1787/eag-2014-en (accessed 10 March 2015).

Riley, R. (2013) Modelling demand for low skilled/low paid labour: exploring the employment trade-offs of a living wage. NIESR Discussion Paper 404.

Schmitt, J. (2013) *Why Does the Minimum Wage Have No Discernible Effect on Employment?* Washington, DC: Center for Economic and Policy Research.

Schultz, T. and Mwabu, G. (1998) Labor unions and the distribution of wages and employment in South Africa. *Industrial and Labor Relations Review* 51: 680–703.

Sen, A., Rybzynski, K. and Van De Waal, C. (2011) Teen employment, poverty, and the minimum wage: evidence from Canada. *Labour Economics* 18: 36–47.

Siebert, W. S. (1986) Restrictive practices in South Africa's labour market. *Economic Affairs* October–November: 26–29.

Siebert, W. S. (2014) The living wage. *Economic Affairs Magazine* Summer: 18–21.

Van der Horst, S. (1942) *Native Labour in South Africa*. London: Frank Cass.

Visser, J. (2013) Wage bargaining institutions – from crisis to crisis. Directorate-General for Economic and Financial Affairs: Economic Papers 488, Brussels.

Wang, J. and Gunderson, M. (2012) Minimum wage effects on employment and wages: dif-in-dif estimates from eastern China. *International Journal of Manpower* 33: 860–76.

5 THE FLAWS IN RENT CEILINGS

Ryan Bourne

Introduction

Rent controls refer to government restrictions on the amount a landlord can charge a tenant for accommodation. They are the best researched and understood form of price control in economics, though the type of controls implemented by governments has undergone various mutations over the past century (Arnott 1997; Jenkins 2009).

Simple controls on rents were implemented in many countries during and after periods of war in the 20th century to prevent alleged profiteering by landlords (Heath 2013). Unsurprisingly, they proved more difficult to abolish than to implement.

These 'first-generation' rent controls in effect create 'rent ceilings' beyond which landlords are unable to increase rents. As such, they only create shortages of rental accommodation if they are set below the market-clearing rent level. A wide range of theoretical and empirical evidence suggests that in practice they did just that, with many other negative unintended consequences (Jenkins 2009).

Over time, these crude controls were therefore abandoned. More recently 'second-generation' controls have been proposed. These are more complex, limiting increases in rent levels alongside other forms of regulation of the landlord–tenant relationship (Arnott 1997). Such controls are often referred to using the more benign sounding phrase 'rent regulation'. Though less damaging than 'first-generation' rent controls, they still have harmful consequences.

The most recent manifestation of this type of regulation has been so-called 'tenancy rent controls'. In the UK, these have recently been proposed by the Labour Party. Under this framework, rent increases would be limited within tenancies but could adjust between tenancies. It is also proposed that the length of the tenancy will be fixed – in the UK case, at three years. While not having as devastating consequences as cruder rent controls, these are still likely to have significant negative costs for the private rental market.

First-generation rent controls

Theory

In a recent survey, 95 per cent of economists disagreed with the proposition that rent control had a positive impact on the amount and quality of broadly affordable rental housing.[1] This is a rare consensus among academic economists. Lindbeck (1971) once went as far as saying: 'In many cases rent control appears to be the most efficient technique presently known to destroy a city – except for bombing'.

A ceiling on rents below the market-clearing level leads to a fall in the quantity of rental property available and a reduction in the quality of the existing stock. Unlike in a competitive market, rent controls negate the ability of the price mechanism to allocate supply given the level of demand – resulting in shortages when rent controls are binding (see Figure 3 in Chapter 2). Holding down rents both increases demand and decreases supply, thus creating a shortage.

---

1   IGM Economic Experts Panel. http://www.igmchicago.org/igm-economic-experts
-panel/poll-results?SurveyID=SV_6upyzeUpI73V5k0 (accessed 10 March 2015).

However, many have argued that a competitive market framework is the wrong way to think about the private rental market (Dillow 2013). Instead it is suggested that landlords have a degree of market power given the very specific demands of tenants and strongly differentiated properties. This could mean that it is more accurate to think of the rented sector as having monopolistic tendencies (Arnott 1997). Rents would then be set above the marginal cost of supplying the property in a free market – creating a monopoly rent for the landlord. If landlords of rentable property believe that withholding supply would increase the price, then a well-designed rent control programme could actually increase the supply of rentable properties by removing the connection between the price achieved in the market and the amount of accommodation supplied by the landlord.

Determining which framework is closer to the truth is ultimately an empirical question. Academic work has suggested that some rental markets can be uncompetitive when viewed through the traditional prism of market concentration or examining the elasticity of supply of rentable accommodation. We might expect the supply of rentable accommodation to be more responsive to changes in price in a competitive market. But the fact that it is not may not be due to monopolistic market practice, but because of regulatory restrictions on land use reducing the housing supply more broadly (Saiz 2008; OECD 2011). Indeed, Malpezzi and Maclennan (2001) show that supply is much more elastic in the US relative to the UK. In the former, land-use planning is much less restrictive. To the extent that rental markets are uncompetitive then, this is often down to policy-induced regulations.

Given this, it is difficult to see how rent controls would help. If the rents obtained by owners of an artificially constrained resource are due to regulation, then the owners might still be operating in a competitive environment in the sense they are unable to determine the market price. Even if land-use planning regulations prevent building in general and keep rents and property prices higher, capping increases in rents just provides landlords with an incentive to sell property that they otherwise might have let or convert properties so that their tenure type falls outside the rent control framework.

Furthermore, when reviewing the literature on first-generation rent control, Arnott (1997) concluded that the 'cumulative evidence – both quantitative and qualitative – strongly supports the predictions of the textbook [competitive] model' and, it might be added, leads to a host of other negative unintended consequences. If rent controls bind, theory would tell us that landlords would have the option to react by cutting investment in the property market, shifting investment into areas where there are no rent controls or allowing properties to fall into disrepair. We would also expect that a sustained suppression of rents below market clearing levels would lead to a progressively deteriorating rental property market. This is exactly what economists have found.

Shortages of rental property

A clear example of the damage caused by rent control can be seen from Britain's experience. Rent control was first introduced in Britain during wartime (1915). Far from being a temporary measure, however, rent controls in some form or another were maintained right through to 1989. In the 1920s landlords were depicted as 'bloodsuckers, profiteers and despots' (Kemp 2004) and, following slight relaxations, the Rent Act 1939 reintroduced full rent control to virtually all rented housing.

By the 1950s rents were fixed either by the 1915 or by the 1939 acts, while tenants could not legally be required to leave. This left many landlords with little incentive to maintain their properties. Yet, for tenants, there was every incentive to remain in their properties given the cheap rents (even when their economic or family circumstances may have made it desirable for them to move on). This was a direct cause of the behaviour of the infamous landlord

Peter Rachman, who would use intimidation, noise and neglect of the upkeep of his accommodation in order to attempt to drive tenants out of properties he wished to sell (Bartholomew 2004). By incentivising tenants to leave, he could sell the property 'with vacant possession'. Unsurprisingly, the amount of rentable accommodation under rent control collapsed.

There were various small changes to the regulations in the post-war period. In 1965 the Rent Act introduced regulated tenancies (with long-term security of tenure) and 'fair rents' assessed by independent officers for tenancies with non-resident landlords. These 'fair rents' were decided by rent officers based on the characteristics of the property. The officer had to explicitly ignore the scarcity of comparable accommodation in the area and the personal characteristics of the tenants. The rent was not based on any economic or rate of return considerations and was very vulnerable to high inflation (Coleman 1988). This exacerbated shortages by keeping rents below market levels in areas where there was already high demand for property, perhaps because of binding land-use planning constraints.

The system was eventually deregulated in 1989. The private rented sector had collapsed from over three-quarters of the housing stock in 1918 to close to one-tenth by the late 1980s and early 1990s (Coleman 1988). This trend can be seen in Figure 10.

Though this is likely to have been in part due to rising incomes and the demand for owner occupation, the advantages in the tax system for mortgage-financed home ownership and the huge expansion of social housing after World War II, it is striking that, after deregulation in 1989, since when new private lettings have generally been somewhat deregulated, the private rented sector has rebounded. In 2013 it comprised 16.5 per cent of the housing stock.

Similar case studies of the negative effects of rent control on the quantity of controlled private rented accommodation have been found in Israel (Werczberger 1988) and Vienna (Hayek 1930).

Figure 10 Trends in tenure (proportion of total households)

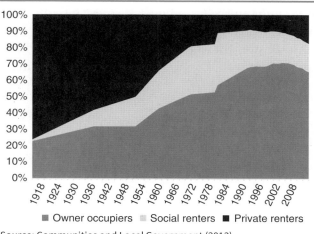

Source: Communities and Local Government (2013).

Friedman and Stigler (1946) perhaps outlined the clearest example when examining San Francisco. In 1906 (when there was a free market in rents), they said, 'the San Francisco Chronicle listed three "houses for sale" for every 10 "houses or apartments for rent". In 1946, under rent control, about 730 "houses for sale" were listed for every 10 "houses or apartments for rent"'.

While, theoretically, rent controls could lead to an increase in the supply of low-quality property for poor people, due to deterioration of higher-quality properties, most of the literature in this area agrees that rent controls reduce the incentive to build by holding down the potential profits from development – and, coupled with the other regulations associated with rent control, increases the cost of capital for investors. This sometimes led to conversion of existing rentable properties to individually owned flats or office space, thus reducing the supply of rentable accommodation further (Mengle 1985).

Empirical evidence on the effects of controls on the stock of rentable housing is unambiguously negative. Two studies on Massachusetts, for example, found that the share of renter-occupied private units in the total housing stock in Cambridge fell from 75 per cent in 1970 to 66 per cent in 1980 under rent control, while in Boston the end of rent control increased the probability that a unit would be a rental unit by 6 percentage points (Navarro 1985; Sims 2007).

Quality and extent of disrepair

Economic theory would also suggest that rent control over a sustained period of time would lead to a deterioration in the quality of rental property (Kutty 1996). After all, there is little incentive for a landlord to maintain a high-quality property if it is let below its market price. One might expect them to allow the quality of property to deteriorate to compensate for the lower rent. This prediction is more difficult to test empirically because of the compensatory impact of self-maintenance by tenants and other regulations which seek to protect tenants against maintenance failure, but there is some evidence. Work on New York's old rent control system, for example, found that there was almost a 9 per cent higher probability of an older or smaller building being in unsound condition in Manhattan if it was in the rent-controlled sector (Gyourko and Linneman 1988). In the UK the long-term effect of rent controls was severe disrepair – with 18 per cent of rentable accommodation defined as unfit and needing repair (Todd et al. 1982). International evidence also shows that countries with more restrictive rent controls have a higher proportion of tenants living in accommodation with a leaky roof (OECD 2011).

Misallocation

The under-supply of rentable properties is a key consequence of rents being held below market rates over a period of time. But any analysis in this area is not complete without considering the cost of the misallocation of property. In the absence of a price mechanism to allocate the rental property to those who value it highest, the allocation of property becomes economically inefficient.

Glaeser and Luttmer (1997) outline three mechanisms through which rent control has economic costs as a result of the misallocation of resources. Firstly, rent controls can distort the relative prices of renting accommodation so that, for example, the cost of luxury accommodation is reduced to a greater extent than that of poor quality accommodation. Secondly, the methods used to allocate apartments, given the excess demand when rents are held below market rates, can be inefficient: because of the potential economic gain associated with securing a property at below market rents, tenants end up searching for longer for accommodation which has an economic opportunity cost. Finally, rents below market levels create significant moving costs and incentives for tenants to stay for longer in properties than they would have done in their absence. In addition, under rent control there is less incentive for families to reduce their accommodation demands, therefore exacerbating the shortage of properties for others.

These misallocation effects are significant. For example, Glaeser and Luttmer (2003) find that 21 per cent of rent-controlled renters in New York live in properties with more rooms or fewer rooms than they would let in a free market. Those living in rent-controlled accommodation are found to be much less mobile than those in non-controlled accommodation (Gyourko and Linneman 1989; Nagy 1995). And more recent analysis even shows that those in rent-controlled sectors are willing to endure much longer commutes to work (Krol and Svorny 2005), suggesting – as theory would predict – that charging below market rents creates a lock-in effect. Indeed, many argued this was a significant structural problem in the UK during the high unemployment period in the 1980s (Minford et al. 1987).

Other considerations

'First-generation' rent controls were often justified as being pro-poor measures that made renting 'more affordable' and often to prevent segregation of rich and poor families. Yet these arguments do not stand up to scrutiny. There is no obvious evidence that rent levels are lower in countries with stricter rent controls (OECD 2011). Whether rent controls are good for the poor depends on how property is allocated in the absence of the price mechanism. There is simply no guarantee that the people who will obtain the benefit of the below-market rent will be poor, and some evidence from Boston and New York suggests the effects were not well-targeted (Sims 2007; Ault and Saba 1990). In fact, with rent control, land-lords have greater incentives to search for tenants who will make their properties more attractive in other ways. This might lead to a pro-rich bias, as landlords seek tenants considered 'easier' to deal with. The queuing effects created by below-market rents may also lead to cronyism, extensive use of existing contacts, or maybe discrimination, side payments and bribes, which could actually worsen segregation between rich and poor (Glaeser 2002). In the UK system, students were favoured because they were less likely to abuse security of tenure provisions. Furthermore, arrangements that also provided board (food) were not included in the framework and thus the provision of such services was artificially encouraged.

Second-generation rent controls

Introduction and theory

Unsurprisingly, few commentators now advocate the sort of crude controls that were seen in Britain and elsewhere (though some do: see Dorling 2014). Instead there are calls for 'second-generation' rent controls, in particular in the form of 'tenancy rent controls'.

Second-generation controls encompass a wide range of different regulatory requirements. They most often entail rules governing increases in rents (rather than the level of rents). Increases may be linked to a rate of inflation or to the average increase in market rents for a particular locality, and they often involve allowing rent increases under certain conditions where it is necessary for landlords to pass through cost increases or undertake investment in a property.

UK proposals for tenancy rent controls

The most recent mutation, as advocated by the Labour party in the UK, is for what could be referred to as 'tenancy rent controls'. These have all the features of second-generation rent controls but allow the landlord complete freedom to adjust rents between tenancies. As such, some suggest they are not really rent controls at all, but could be better described as longer-term, fixed-price contracts. Since rents would be free to adjust between tenancies, they do not have the same consequences as first-generation rent controls. Ultimately, rents will be determined by supply and demand, at least at the beginning of a tenancy. This means that they do not lead to the progressively worsening outcomes seen with 'first-generation' rent controls over time (Arnott 2003). Instead it is best to think of them as protection for tenants against the possibility of large, unforeseen rent increases within a tenancy. This explains why tenancy rent controls are often accompanied by security of tenure arrangements.

Earlier, David Lammy MP had pressed for rent controls along German lines. In Germany, rents are free to be set according to market conditions between tenancies, but tenants enjoy indefinite tenancies during which rents can only be increased by a maximum of 20 per cent in any three-year period (Lammy 2013). Too many renters in London, according to Lammy, were faced with uncertain and unaffordable rents within the current framework. The homeless charity Shelter and other campaigning organisations such as Generation Rent have expressed similar concerns about the uncertainty of renting, and have thus called for moves to make tenancies more secure. Indeed, the Secretary of State for the Department of Communities and Local Government, Eric Pickles MP, while not proposing statutory implementation, had proposed to work with the industry to draw up more secure 'model contracts' with inflation-linked rents – suggesting that even the coalition government had begun thinking along these lines (DCLG 2013).

The figures on annual rents in the UK are indeed stark. Average rent levels across the country for those in the private rented sector are equivalent to 41.1 per cent of weekly gross household income (ONS & DCLG 2013). Even among local authority and housing association homes, the figure is 29.6 per cent. This is after taking into consideration state assistance in the form of housing benefit as part of gross weekly income, the annual bill for which now stands at £23.9 billion (DWP 2014). Excluding this benefit, the average proportion of the remaining weekly household income going on rents from private and 'social' renters would be as much as 50.7 per cent and 40.4 per cent respectively (ONS & DCLG 2013). London has extraordinarily high rent levels. The Valuation Office Agency calculates that the median monthly rent for two-bedroom accommodation in London is £1,387: more than double the average for England. Annual incomes in London are only 39 per cent higher.

The homeless charity Shelter has proposed that regulations for more secure tenure would be good for both tenants and landlords, particularly in difficult economic times. With over 1.3 million households in the UK now renting, Shelter's polling claims that 66 per cent of private renters would like to have the option to stay in their tenancy longer and 79 per cent would like to know that their landlord/letting agents would not be able to raise their rent above a certain rate while they were living in the property.

This is perhaps unsurprising – tenants will always value flexibility. But those in favour of longer tenancies underpinned by state legislation also claim that the sorts of assured shorthold tenancies that dominate the UK rental market are only so prevalent because both landlords and tenants are trapped in a market norm, from which they would both prefer to move away. Long-term contracts are held up as being more successful and it is argued that more security of tenure would be good for landlords, who would enjoy lower vacancy risk.

The actual proposals put forward by the Labour Party did not go as far as the rent control model seen in Germany. Rather than indefinite tenancies, Labour proposes new fixed three-year tenancies during which a landlord can evict a tenant only for breach of contract (such as arrears or anti-social behaviour) or because the landlord needs the property for their family or to sell. While there would be complete freedom for landlords to set rents between tenancies, rents within tenancies would be benchmarked so that increases will be linked to average increases within a locality, some measure of inflation, or both.[2] These changes would give an option to tenants, who would still be able to terminate their contract after the probationary period with one month's notice.

Do tenancy rent controls improve affordability or security?

Tenancy rent control cannot improve the affordability of renting in general but only in the short term. They can protect existing tenants from large rent rises within tenancies, and as such from landlord attempts to drive someone out of a tenancy by increasing rents (sometimes called 'economic eviction').

At its least harmful, tenancy rent control is just likely to change the timing of the overall rent cost within a tenancy (Nagy 1997).

---

2   The party has asked The Royal Institute of Chartered Surveyors to review the most appropriate benchmark.

Since landlords know they cannot adjust rents each year to fully reflect market conditions, they are likely to set rents at the start of the tenancy according to their judgement as to the expected market rents over the lifetime of the tenancy. If they expect that the market rent will increase by more than the average used to determine the rent control, they will front-load the rent level to compensate for their future loss. When landlords expect market rents to bind, new tenants are likely to face higher rents initially than they would in a free market in order to compensate for forecast lower future rents than there would otherwise have been.

Since the major effect on returns to the landlord from tenancy rent control is to change the timing within a tenancy, we should not expect the same dramatic effects on investment in rental housing construction and the supply of rentable property as we had from rent control in the 20th century.

Nevertheless, there will almost certainly be a fall in investment in the private rented sector if tenancy rent control is viewed as a precursor to even more regulation in future. In addition, given that any form of rent control restricts the landlords' ability to manage their risks, in all probability there is likely to be a small negative effect on investment due to an increased cost of capital and/or a small rise in the overall rents to reflect the greater risk. This means the overall market rents are likely to increase slightly if tenancy rent controls are introduced. In effect, an option is being given to the tenant (if market rents increase rapidly, the tenant will not face rent increases as high as market rent increases and if market rents fall or increase slowly, the tenant can expect a reduction in rent). Such options come with a cost and with risks to landlords.

Many people claim that tenancy rent controls are necessary in order to improve the security of tenure for tenants, which is said to have desirable economic consequences. The implicit assumption here is that there is some sort of market failure in the rental property market whereby both landlords and tenants would benefit from regulation to ensure that tenancies are more secure. The vision often painted is of a young family with children who would like the security of knowing they have a guaranteed fixed-term rental contract limiting exceptional increases in rent and the threat of economic eviction. From the landlord's perspective, it is assumed that the threat of vacancy is a significant consideration, and that by changing the market norms via fixed-term contracts, this vacancy risk can be more effectively managed.

Is this justified? And to what extent do tenancy rent controls affect tenure security? In the UK there is very little evidence that tenure security is unavailable when tenants are willing to pay for it (Ball 2013). Longer-term tenancies with more stability and predictable rents do exist, but are not widely taken up. Shelter and other campaigners use evidence that tenants say that they would like more security of tenure to justify their market failure arguments. But the truth would appear to be that tenants are unwilling to pay for increased security.

From the perspective of the landlord, an additional problem is the asymmetric nature of the tenancy agreements that have been proposed. For example, the proposals would mean that tenants could leave a property with one month's notice while landlords could only evict tenants for breach of contract within the three-year period.

In a free market, with no regulated fixed-period agreements, a landlord could seek to impose penalties within a contract for early termination by the tenant to compensate him for vacancy risk. Indeed, contrary to the narrative that secure tenancies dissipate vacancy risk for landlords, these types of controls actually force landlords to bear the vacancy risk – and do not allow them to use market mechanisms currently in operation when the preferences of landlords and their tenants align (Ball 2013). On top of this, landlords in a secure tenancy framework would face the prospect of problem tenants enjoying greater security of tenure, making the management of risk through turnover more difficult.

As has been noted, it is unclear that there is a significant security of tenure problem in the UK. Although survey data do suggest people would like more secure arrangements, the fact that the private rental market is dominated by the young, mobile and childless demographic groups suggest that security of tenure might not be a huge problem in practice (see Table 7). Not only is there little evidence that private renting tenants are unhappy with their accommodation per se (according to the English Housing Survey, overall satisfaction rates were at 91.2 per cent in 2011–12) or that many people move involuntarily, but there is also little evidence that even parents with children are substantially less mobile than other renters (Ball 2013). For example, the English Housing Survey shows 18.9 per cent of households with dependent children moved within the last year, compared with 23.7 per cent without. At least part of the reason for this is because many rent as a stepping stone to owner occupation: 24.8 per cent of new owner occupiers over the past three years were households with dependent children who were previously in rented accommodation.

The existence of controls may also affect decisions of landlords and tenants in the allocation of rental properties, both prior to and within a tenancy. Since landlords

Table 7 Economic and demographic characteristics of private market renters

Age	Proportion
16–34	53.0%
35–54	35.6%
55+	11.4%

Marital status	Proportion
Single	32.1%
Married	27.0%
Cohabiting	23.5%
Other	17.4%

Number of persons in household	Proportion
One	25.1%
Two	37.7%
Three	19.4%
Four	10.9%
5+	5.1%

Household type	Proportion
No dependent children	65.7%
Dependent children	34.3%

Length of residence	Proportion
< 1 year	35.4%
1–3 years	36.7%
3–5 years	13.8%
5+ years	14.2%

Source: English Housing Survey (2013), Table FA3101 (S418): Demographic and economic characteristics of social and privately renting households, 2011–12.

with properties who expect the rent controls to bind are likely to front-load their rent levels, landlords face an incentive to seek out tenants who are likely to be mobile, such as students or young people (Arnott 2003). This is because the early years of the tenancy are when the landlord makes the highest profit.

Within tenancies, landlords are likely to have an incentive to speed up a tenant's departure the longer the tenant stays in the property if the rent control binds. This might express itself as being less cooperative to the tenant as time goes on, or by being less willing to undertake maintenance. The opposite incentives apply for the tenant. If a tenant's situation changes, for example, as a result of a job offer, he is less likely – all else given – to move given the benefit of a lower real rent later in the existing tenancy relative to starting a new tenancy. This might mean either a longer commute or a reduced likelihood of the tenant taking the job. Tenancy rent controls therefore benefit less mobile households to the detriment of more mobile households and are likely to have a negative effect on mobility.

The existence of tenancy rent controls and contracts is also likely to change the timing of when maintenance occurs. Landlords are much more likely to undertake maintenance between tenancies than within them. This is particularly true if market rents increase more quickly than the landlord expected prior to the tenancy agreement. Tenants are also likely to have to undertake more self-maintenance on a property than they would in an uncontrolled market within a tenancy (Olsen 1988). With tenancy rent control inevitably comes an expansion of bureaucracy too – and this will also have a vested interest in more regulation.

But don't rents controls work in Germany?

Many advocates of tenancy rent controls argue that they work in other countries such as Germany (Lammy 2013). In Germany, rents are set by the market initially but then can be raised within tenancies with reference to inflation or increases in the land-lord's costs. Rents cannot increase by more than 20 per cent in any three-year period. Tenants have indefinite tenancies and can only be evicted for non-payment of rent (over a number of months), for breach of contract arising from damage to the property, for unauthorised subletting, or to allow the landlord or a member of his family to live in the home or to allow the landlord to sell the home.

Attributing the success of the German rental market to 'tenancy rent controls', however, ignores huge structural differences in the housing market more broadly compared with the UK. In particular, the fact that there is a much more elastic supply response to changes in the demand for housing in Germany due to more liberal land-use planning regulations, means that both rents and house prices are much lower relative to income than in the UK (Niemietz 2014). Figure 11 shows that affordability of German housing has continually improved since 1980, whereas for the UK the reverse is true. This is largely caused by significantly higher levels of dwelling completion per 10,000 inhabitants in

Figure 11 House price to average income ratio in Germany and UK (1980 Q1 = 100)

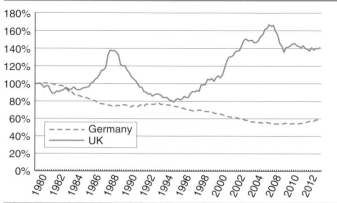

Table 8   Comparison of rent levels in UK and German cities, 2014

Rent per month	London	Munich	Manchester	Frankfurt
Apartment (1 bedroom) in city centre	£1,502.28	£699.54	£636.22	£530.63
Apartment (1 bedroom) outside of centre	£945.41	£558.66	£468.33	£351.79
Apartment (3 bedrooms) in city centre	£2,837.50	£1,395.04	£1,155.00	£1,061.48
Apartment (3 bedrooms) outside of centre	£1,720.18	£997.13	£836.00	£762.44
Average monthly disposable salary (after tax)	£2,100.08	£1,880.02	£1,253.48	£2,518.04

Rent per month	Birmingham	Berlin	Oxford	Hamburg
Apartment (1 bedroom) in city centre	£632.14	£477.11	£987.50	£526.83
Apartment (1 bedroom) outside of centre	£432.86	£344.20	£768.00	£407.30
Apartment (3 bedrooms) in city centre	£1,150.00	£992.74	£1,638.80	£1,381.71
Apartment (3 bedrooms) outside of centre	£700.00	£698.89	£1,283.33	£717.85
Average monthly disposable salary (after tax)	£1,755.62	£1,458.67	£1,700.00	£1,660.30

Source: Numbeo, Property prices comparison between Berlin and London, averages.

Germany compared with the UK (Niemietz 2014; Ball 2013). Unsurprisingly then, rent levels are lower. Table 8 shows rent levels in UK and German cities according to the cost-of-living comparison website Numbeo.

The structural differences which make rent levels much higher in UK cities make every other consideration relatively trivial – it is unsurprising that the effects of tenancy rent controls in Germany look benign when other factors are making renting much more affordable compared with the UK.

That said, some recent studies have suggested problems developing in the German rental property market in terms of low levels of investment in new development, with rents rising as a result (Ball 2013). In fact, in many cases where long-term contracts and tenancy rent controls operate, the rental markets suffer from low levels of investment. This has led to other policy responses such as more support for new development, allowances and tax breaks. Any comparison must take into account these different frameworks. The OECD also suggests that the proportion of rentable accommodation with a leaky roof is much higher in Germany (over 7 per cent) than the UK at 1.5 per cent (OECD 2011).

Conclusion

Rent control is back on the agenda, particularly in the UK, because of the cost-of-living squeeze, structurally high rent levels and a large housing benefits bill. The sort of crude controls of nominal rents implemented and maintained by many Western countries following periods of war in the 20th century have long been abandoned as a policy ambition. These are recognised to have devastating consequences on the supply and maintenance of rentable property, while having large economic costs associated with resource misallocation and reduced labour mobility.

Instead, many policymakers now advocate a variation of 'second-generation' rent controls, known as tenancy rent controls, in which landlords are free to adjust rent levels between tenancies but are restricted within them. In the UK, for example, the Labour party wants fixed three-year tenancies where rents can only be raised by an as yet unspecified 'average' rental increase.

Tenancy rent controls by construction cannot improve affordability and they may raise market rents. Their use entails a trade-off between providing more secure tenure for existing tenants against the economic inefficiency caused by reduced labour mobility, and the potential for lower investment in the rentable housing stock.

As such, though not as damaging as first-generation rent controls, it is unlikely that rent controls will achieve the desired aims of improved affordability and substantial security for tenants. The real problem here is the affordability of housing. A more flexible supply enabled by a liberalisation of planning is the type of policy we should be following, rather than imposing new conditions on a market which has been a relative success story since liberalisation in 1989.

Indeed, planning liberalisation would clearly be a welfare enhancing policy, while tenancy rent controls would not. As with most price ceilings, if they are effective in reducing tenants' costs and/or increasing security (which is highly unlikely), they will do a great deal of damage. If they do not do much damage, they will not reduce costs or increase tenant security noticeably. Of course, these proposed price ceilings – as with more radical measures implemented in the 20th century – do provide a readily observable policy to show that politicians are 'acting' on the concerns of interest groups with any negative consequences likely to be opaque. The policies are more likely to be in the interests of those who propose them than in the interests of those whom they are purported to benefit.

References

Andrews, D., Johansson, A. and Sanchez, A. (2011) Housing markets and structural policies in OECD countries. OECD Working Paper 836.

Arnott, R. (1997) *Rent Control*. The New Palgrave Dictionary of Economics and the Law. London: Palgrave Macmillan.

Arnott, R. (2003) Tenancy rent control. Swedish Economic Policy Review 10.

Ault, R. and Saba, R. (1990) The economic effects of long-term rent control: the case of New York. *Journal of Real Estate Finance and Economics* 3(1): 25–41.

Ball, M. (2004) *The Future of Private Renting in the UK*. The Social Market Foundation.

Ball, M. (2013) Why governments should not enforce long-term contracts in the UK's private rented sector. Residential Landlords' Association.

Bartholomew, J. (2004) *The Welfare State We're In*. London: Politico's.

Basu, K. and Emerson, P. (2003) Efficiency pricing, tenancy rent control and monopolistic landlords. *Economica* 70: 223–32.

Cheshire, P. (2014) Why Britain's housing crisis risks turning into catastrophe. *City AM*, 3 June.

Coleman, D. (1988) Rent control: the British experience and policy response. *Journal of Real Estate Finance and Economics* 1(3): 233–55.

Communities and Local Government (2013) FT1101 (S101) Trends in Tenure.

DCLG (2013) Better tenancies for families in rental homes. October.

Dillow, C. (2013) A case for rent control? Stumbling and Mumbling blog. http://stumblingandmumbling.typepad.com/stumbling_and_mumbling/2013/08/a-case-for-rent-control.html (accessed 10 March 2015).

Dorling, D. (2014) *All That Is Solid: The Great Housing Disaster*. London: Penguin.

DWP (2013) Impact of rent growth on housing benefit expenditure.

DWP (2014) Benefit expenditure and caseload tables 2014.

Friedman, M. and Stigler, G. (1957) Roofs or ceilings? The current housing problem. Institute of Economic Affairs: Verdict on Rent Control. http://www.iea.org.uk/publications/research/verdict-on-rent-control (accessed 10 March 2015).

Glaeser, E. (2002) Does rent control reduce segregation? Harvard Institute of Economic Research Discussion Paper 1985.

Glaeser, E. and Luttmer, E. (1997) The misallocation of housing under rent control. NBER Working Paper 6220.

Glaeser, E. and Luttmer, E. (2003) The misallocation of housing under rent control. *American Economic Review* 93(4): 1027–46.

Gyourko, J. and Linneman, P. (1988) Rent controls and rental housing quality: a note on the effects of New York City's old controls. *Journal of Urban Economics* 27: 347–72.

Gyourko, J. and Linneman, P. (1989) Equity and efficiency aspects of rent control: an empirical study of New York City. *Journal of Urban Economics* 26(1): 5–74.

Hayek, F. (1957) The repercussions of rent restrictions. Institute of Economic Affairs: Verdict on Rent Control. http://www.iea.org.uk/publications/research/verdict-on-rent-control (accessed 10 March 2015).

Heath, S. (2013) The historical context of rent control in the private rented sector. House of Commons Library Standard Note: SP/6747.

Heath, S. (2014) Rent control in the private rented sector (England). House of Commons Library Standard Note: SP/6760.

Jenkins, B. (2009) Rent control: do economists agree? *Econ Journal Watch* 6(1): 73–112.

Kemp, P. (2004) *Private Renting in Transition*. Chartered Institute of Housing.

Krol, R. and Svorny, S. (2005) The effect of rent control on commute times. *Journal of Urban Economics* 58(3): 421–36.

Kutty, N. (1996) The impact of rent control on housing maintenance: a dynamic analysis incorporating European and North American Rent Regulations. *Housing Studies* 11(1): 69–88.

Lammy, D. (2014) We need rent controls to solve London's housing crisis. *New Statesman*, 27 February.

Lindbeck, A. (1971) *The Political Economy of the New Left: An Outsider's View*. New York: Harper and Row.

Malpezzi, S. and Maclennan, D. (2001) The long-run price elasticity of supply of new residential construction in the United States and the United Kingdom. *Journal of Housing Economics* 10: 278–306.

Mengle, D. (1985) The effect of second generation rent controls on the quality of rental housing. Federal Reserve Bank of Richmond Working Paper 85-5.

Nagy, J. (1997) Do vacancy decontrol provisions undo rent control? *Journal of Urban Economics* 42(1): 64–78.

Navarro, P. (1985) Rent control in Cambridge, Massachusetts. *Public Interest* 78(4): 83–100.

Niemietz, K. (2012) *Abundance of Land, Shortage of Housing.* Institute of Economic Affairs. http://www.iea.org.uk/publications/research/abundance-of-land-shortage-of-housing (accessed 10 March 2015).

Niemietz, K. (2014) Why 'second generation rent controls' are not a solution to the affordability crisis, Part 1. IEA Blog. http://www.iea.org.uk/blog/why-%E2%80%98second-generation-rent-controls%E2%80%99-are-not-a-solution-to-the-affordability-crisis-part-1 (accessed 10 March 2015).

Niemietz, K. (2014) Why 'second generation rent controls' are not a solution to the affordability crisis, Part 2: Beware false comparisons. IEA Blog. http://www.iea.org.uk/blog/why-%E2%80%98second-generation-rent-controls%E2%80%99-are-not-a-solution-to-the-affordability-crisis-part-2-bew (accessed 10 March 2015).

OECD (2011) Housing and the economy: policies for renovation.

Olsen, E. (1988) What do economists know about the effect of rent control on housing maintenance? *Journal of Real Estate Finance and Economics* 1(3): 295–307.

Olsen, E. (1998) Economics of rent control. Regional Science and Urban Economics.

ONS (2013) Annual survey of hours and earnings, 2013. Provisional results.

ONS & DCLG (2013) English housing survey: households 2011–12.

ONS & DCLG (2014) English housing survey 2012 to 2013: headline report.

Pennington, M. (2002) *Liberating the Land.* London: Institute of Economic Affairs. http://www.iea.org.uk/publications/research/liberating-the-land-the-case-for-private-land-use-planning (accessed 10 March 2015).

Saiz, A. (2008) On local housing supply elasticity. Working paper, The Wharton School.

Shelter (2013) The rent trap and the fading dream of owning a home. January.

Sims, D. (2007) Out of control: what can we learn from the end of Massachusetts rent control? *Journal of Urban Economics* 61(1): 129–51.

Sims, D. (2008) Rent control rationing, community composition, and residential segregation. 2009 AEA Annual Meeting in San Francisco.

Valuation Office Agency (2013) Private rental market statistics.

Werczberger, E. (1988) The experience with rent control in Israel: from rental housing to condominiums. *Journal of Real Estate Finance and Economics* 1(3): 277–93.

Wilson, W. (2014) The fair rent regime. House of Commons Library Standard Note: SP/638.

6 ENERGY PRICE CAPS

Colin Robinson

Price controls have often been applied in energy markets, whether under state or private ownership, by legislators or by government-appointed regulators. They are back on the political agenda in the UK after a statement by the leader of the Labour Party in autumn 2013 that, if Labour were elected in 2015, it would impose a two-year freeze on gas and electricity prices. Mr Miliband's proposal is only the latest intimation of a profound change in the UK energy market, which, ten years ago, could claim to be the most liberalised in the world. Subsequently, competitive forces have weakened and government and regulatory controls have tightened. Not only is political action on prices threatened but, over the last few years, the gas and electricity regulator, Ofgem, has been tampering with retail tariffs in the interests of 'fairness' and 'simplicity'.

This chapter considers the consequences of substituting prices determined by politicians or regulators for those that would otherwise have appeared through the free interaction of consumers and producers. It begins with some observations on the price mechanism, considers past attempts at price control in the UK before and after privatisation, and discusses, within the context of recent changes in the UK energy market, the likely consequences of attempts by governments and government-appointed regulators to influence or determine energy prices.

Markets and price controls

The price mechanism

The price mechanism has a vital role in all forms of markets. As a decentralised system, it incorporates and processes very large amounts of information without the need for any central guiding hand, and it provides signals to producers and consumers which permit scarce supplies to be allocated among competing uses at any point in time.[1] It is a sophisticated adaptive system which incorporates views about the future, providing (via variations in prices and price expectations which lead to supply and demand changes) for constant adjustment over time to incipient shortages and surpluses. Without the price mechanism there would be no competitive markets, which provide the driving force for the process of competitive discovery that stimulates innovation (Hayek 1948) and which, by permitting choice of suppliers, are the prime means of protection for consumers. Given the fundamental nature of the price mechanism, attempts by governments and regulators to fix prices are clearly likely to have profound consequences. Prices themselves can be controlled, at least for short periods, but the market effects of controls cannot be so easily managed.

Price controls and the price mechanism

Prices may be capped by a regulator or a government because suppliers are thought likely to exploit a monopoly. Or the cap may be because a government wants to keep down the rate of inflation as measured by published consumer price indices. Or a government may want some key products to be provided at low prices for consumers, as for instance in oil-producing countries,

---

1 The characteristics of capitalist systems, including the role of the price mechanism, are particularly well set out in Seldon (1990).

where governments have sometimes used subsidies to hold down oil product prices so that their citizens feel they are obtaining benefits from local resources.

Price caps may be justified when there is clear evidence that an organisation is exploiting market power, though a better corrective is to undermine that market power by removing barriers to entry to the relevant activity. Nevertheless, the fundamental problem with using price controls as a 'remedy' is that it involves tampering with one of the basic mechanisms of the economy even though the government or regulator involved can have very little relevant knowledge of what prices 'should' be. Attempts to fix prices invariably upset the allocative and signalling functions of markets and lead to unforeseen consequences (which may not greatly concern politicians and regulators because they may not appear in the short term). Compared with the situation that would otherwise have existed, a price cap that is effective will, in any likely circumstances, result in increased demand and reduced supply at the controlled price level, thus creating a situation of excess demand in which prices try to rise but are prevented from doing so by government or regulatory action. In the short run, some kind of rationing will be required since the market will not be in balance at the frozen price level.

Less obviously, the imposition of controls will reduce the incentive to invest: profit expectations will be lowered, both because of the direct effect of lower expected prices and because of increased political uncertainty caused by the intervention. The threat of a price cap (even if the cap is never imposed) will have much the same effect. In other words, an unintended and perverse consequence of actual or threatened price controls will be to induce shortages, both in the present and in the future, by boosting future demand and restricting future supply. This perverse effect will persist as long as the controls (or the threat of controls) remain: indeed it may persist longer if perceived political and regulatory risk is increased.[2]

Past attempts at price control

Before privatisation

In the UK during World War II, the price mechanism was suppressed in many markets and administrative rationing was substituted to deal with the associated shortages. It was well into the 1950s before these controls were eased. Subsequently, given the then consensus about macroeconomic policy and the high rates of inflation that developed, governments of both major political parties tried, with little success, to intervene in markets to hold down prices and incomes. Prices and incomes policies, which attempted to persuade unions to rein back wage demands and employers to minimise price increases, were particularly popular with governments in the 1960s and 1970s.

In the case of energy prices, governments had a degree of control since the gas, electricity and coal industries were nationalised just after the end of World War II. Conflicts between nationalised corporation boards and government about objectives and actions to achieve those objectives (including price setting) were common (Heald 1980) and governments frequently intervened by backdoor means to influence or even fix prices in the energy and other state-owned industries. Since so much of this activity went on behind the scenes, its scale is not entirely clear. Nevertheless, at times, it came out into the open. For example, in the 1970s,

---

2 A further damaging effect of price caps in energy markets could occur if a number of countries capped prices at the same time. In those circumstances, the effects could feed into markets for depletable primary energy products where producers might well assume that they should hold back supplies until prices rose in the future. The relevant theory of depletable resources is explained in Krautkraemer (1998). The rest of this chapter assumes that the UK is alone in capping prices.

Harold Wilson's government discussed and determined gas and electricity prices in Cabinet, holding them below the levels the nationalised corporations wished to charge because of concern about the impact of increasing gas and electricity prices on the retail prices index. It was not only Labour governments that interfered with nationalised industry prices. Before privatisation of the major utilities began in 1984,[3] Margaret Thatcher's government intervened, but on that occasion it was (indirectly) to raise prices higher than the industries concerned wanted rather than to cap them. When government borrowing was soaring in the early 1980s, the 1983 Autumn Statement increased repayments by the nationalised gas and electricity industries to the government, making them raise the prices they charged their consumers (Marshall and Robinson 1984).

By the later 1980s, however, as the old consensus about centralised direction of the economy faded and monetary policy was recognised as the main instrument in controlling inflation, prices and incomes policies disappeared from the policy agenda. Furthermore, once many of the nationalised corporations were privatised and independent regulators were established, direct government interference in their pricing decisions became more difficult so that one favoured conduit for government price interference was blocked.

Post privatisation

However, price controls of a different sort then became popular. Along with privatisation of the utilities came a new form of regulation, including price controls, which was fortunately relatively benign because it was operated by regulators with duties to promote competition (Robinson and Marshall 2006). As far as prices were concerned, the regulators of the newly privatised utilities

---

3   The first was the sale of 50 per cent of British Telecommunications in 1984.

used a price cap based on general movements in retail prices but with a specific element for each industry. The RPI-X formula tied prices in an industry to the change in the general retail prices index (RPI) but minus a specific deduction for efficiency improvements (X) (Beesley and Littlechild 1983).[4]

The underlying idea of these controls, which were advocated by those who wished to liberalise markets, was that an RPI-X price cap was justified in either one of two sets of circumstances. One was that the regulators, in pursuit of their duties to promote competition, needed to cap prices temporarily in 'pre-competitive markets': that is, markets which were potentially competitive but which were not yet actually so. These controls were to be transitional, aimed at curbing temporary market power, and would be dropped as soon as effective competition had been achieved. In Beesley and Littlechild's phrase, RPI-X was intended to 'hold the fort' until competition arrived.

Another justification for controls was in 'naturally monopolistic' sectors of the industries – in the case of energy, the networks of pipes and wires that carry energy from where it is produced to where it is consumed – where it was thought unlikely, short of some unexpected technological change, that competition would be feasible and efficient. These price caps on natural monopoly areas were conceived as permanent and necessary to prevent beneficiaries of a natural monopoly from exploiting their market power to the detriment of others. RPI-X was expected to provide better efficiency incentives than the main alternative which was US-style cost-plus regulation, which had a tendency to inflate costs and promote investment-intensity.[5]

---

4 In the case of water, prices were allowed to rise faster than RPI.

5 Under the US system, regulated companies were permitted to earn a percentage rate of return on their allowable costs (the 'rate base'). Thus they had an incentive to inflate the rate base to increase their money return (Averch and Johnson 1963). The UK regime has problems of its own, as does any regulatory intervention (see, for example, Crew and Kleindorfer 2006).

In the late 1990s and early 2000s, the energy regulators[6] pursued a successful policy of separating the natural monopoly networks from the potentially competitive sectors (a separation which had not been done at the time of privatisation in gas and not fully done in the case of electricity), as a precondition for the introduction of effective competition in all potentially competitive sectors. At the same time, barriers to entry to potentially competitive markets were removed and, as competition began to flourish, price controls were removed. All had gone by 2002, leaving RPI-X as a cap on prices in the natural monopoly networks.

In some other utility markets, the energy regulator's policy of opening markets to competition where feasible and removing price controls was unfortunately not followed. In the water industry in England and Wales, for instance, where prices in the regional monopoly companies were permitted to rise faster than RPI, there was no separation of potentially competitive sectors from the network. In water, privatised in 1989, far from price caps 'holding the fort' until competition arrived (Beesley and Littlechild 1983), prices are still largely set by the regulator. Competition has still not arrived despite some efforts in recent years to introduce it.

Under the benign approach in the energy market, in which the utility regulator promoted competition wherever feasible and only resorted to price controls in other markets where monopoly seemed inevitable, there were considerable benefits for energy consumers, large and small, especially after 1998 when all consumers were given choice of supplier. Providing consumers with the power of exit from suppliers they did not like was a massive step forward, which no other country had taken. There was sufficient rivalry to induce suppliers to reduce and then keep down costs and prices. Domestic consumers who switched supplier

---

6   The original energy regulators (Offer for electricity and Ofgas for gas) were combined in Ofgem in 2000.

typically obtained price reductions of about 20 per cent for gas and 10 per cent for electricity.[7]

The retreat from liberalisation

In more recent times, regulation of the energy utilities has become more interventionist. Competition promotion no longer has the priority it had just before and just after the turn of the century. Detailed government and regulatory interference in prices charged by suppliers has begun and more political interference is threatened. This regression towards pre-privatisation views and actions is best seen in the context of changing government policy towards the energy industries over the period since 1945.

A potted history of UK energy regulation

In the aftermath of World War II, central planning of energy was in vogue, in the UK as elsewhere (see also Robinson 2013, 2014). Coal mining, electricity production, transmission and distribution and gas distribution (of manufactured gas) were in government hands. The oil industry was not nationalised but it was subject to substantial government interference.

However, as liberal market economics staged a revival in the last twenty years of the 20th century, UK governments retreated from their previous efforts to regulate energy markets. As explained above, regulators were encouraged by the privatisation legislation in the 1980s to promote competition outside natural monopoly networks and, for a time, market forces played a much bigger role in UK energy than they had in living memory.[8]

---

7   The National Audit Office and the Comptroller and Auditor General produced reports on gas and electricity liberalisation which argued that the results were generally beneficial for consumers (NAO, 1999 and 2000 and Comptroller and Auditor General 2003).

8   The market was not entirely freed: coal, nuclear power and renewables were subsidised as explained, for example, in Robinson (2006).

This period of liberalisation was very brief. It took time for energy regulators to establish the conditions for effective competition so that it was the late 1990s before the liberalised market came into being for all consumers and it then lasted less than ten years (Robinson 2014). By the early years of the 21st century government energy planning had staged a comeback. The Blair government initially supported the introduction of competition but, in its later stages and under Gordon Brown, Labour governments followed in all essentials by the subsequent coalition, claimed that, if energy markets were allowed to operate freely, there would be adverse effects on the natural environment and on energy security. Government must intervene to protect the interests of the community as a whole.[9]

An important consequence was that, as under nationalisation, government again began to play a major part in determining electricity generators' investment programmes. Private generators were induced to use 'renewables' such as wind and biomass, rather than fossil fuels such as gas, and to embark on a new nuclear power programme, passing on the costs to consumers. As explained below, numerous measures were introduced in an attempt to ensure that the energy market developed in line with the wishes of the government of the day. A competitive energy market could not survive this barrage of government initiatives.[10]

Not surprisingly in such circumstances, the objectives of the energy regulator, Ofgem, were changed from 2008 onwards[11] so

---

9 A White Paper in 2007 (DTI 2007) was the first to make explicit the retreat from liberalisation (see Robinson 2014).

10 Robinson (2014) argues that the period of liberalisation was so brief because neither the government nor the principal players in the market wanted a competitive market.

11 First, under the 2008 Energy Act, then in January 2010 when revised social and environmental guidance was issued and in 2011 to align regulation with the government's 'strategic policy goals'. Ofgem's principal objective is now the rather vague 'to protect the interests of existing and future electricity and gas consumers'.

that it no longer gave primacy to competition promotion. An independent competition-promoting regulator could not comfortably coexist with an interventionist government. To keep Ofgem in line, it is now constrained to bring about the government's stated energy strategy and policy as set out in a Strategy and Policy Statement (DECC 2012). The government claims that Ofgem's regulatory independence is not compromised since it is free to decide how to achieve the outcomes specified by government (see DECC 2012, especially paragraphs 13–18). Nevertheless, 'independent' regulation no longer has the same meaning as it did when it formed an important part of the post-privatisation regulatory settlement which was designed to avoid the political interference that had been rife under nationalisation (Robinson and Marshall 2006).

Ofgem and intervention in pricing

'Fairness' and 'simplicity'

The actions of Ofgem in the recent past are consonant with the new interventionist approach (Robinson 2014). Instead of encouraging competition in potentially competitive markets, as did its predecessors, it is regulating those markets and, in particular, trying to micro-manage prices. For example, in 2009 Ofgem introduced a new licence condition intended to ban price differentials between regions and between payment methods that were not justified by cost differences. Ofgem had observed that prices varied between regions and that suppliers were also varying prices according to methods of payment and, after investigation, it judged these differentials to be 'unfair'. The ban on 'unjustified' differentials between payment methods is still in force and, though the formal ban on regional differentials was dropped in 2012, Ofgem has warned that it could take action if 'unjustified' differentials return. Ofgem also introduced a Simple

Tariffs policy in 2013 because it believed that the number of tariffs was so large that consumers were confused. All suppliers were limited to four tariffs per fuel.

As Stephen Littlechild has explained, Ofgem's new price policies have been damaging to consumers. They have had the unintended and perverse consequences of restricting consumer choice and raising prices. Ofgem's attempt to curb differential pricing, by stopping energy companies from charging different prices to in-area and out-of-area consumers,[12] resulted in a decline in differentials but not because of a reduction in prices. Differentials were reduced because out-of-area prices increased: customer switching consequently declined and supplier profits increased. Estimates vary of how much supplier profits have risen, but there is no doubt that the increase is considerable: according to Littlechild, the increase was between £1 and 2 billion per year between 2008 and 2013 (Littlechild 2014c).

More recently, Ofgem's attempts to 'simplify' tariffs have resulted in less choice for consumers and the disappearance of some of the more attractive tariffs, such as those that contain no standing charges and those that give discounts for prompt payment. At the same time, Ofgem is becoming involved in time-consuming decisions about actions which may transgress its 'simple' tariff rules (Littlechild 2014b). These kinds of efforts to persuade or force suppliers to provide only the tariffs the regulator thinks are desirable are only too likely to allow suppliers to discard those tariffs that are less profitable.

The change in Ofgem's approach is extremely significant. The rationale of gas and electricity regulation in the first twenty years or so after gas privatisation was that the regulator should avoid the traditional approach (which had proved so detrimental to consumers under nationalisation) in which the regulator works

---

12 'In-area' refers to former incumbents when operating in their 'home regions', whereas 'out-of-area' refers to their operating as entrants to other regions.

out what outcomes are desirable, including for prices, and then attempts to impose them on the industry. Instead, the regulator should accept that desirable outcomes are unknowable and can be achieved only by the forces of competition: therefore, wherever possible, the regulator's task is to remove entry barriers and promote competition, leaving outcomes beneficial to consumers to emerge from the competitive process. Ofgem's approach in the last few years has moved back towards the traditional, discredited approach in which the regulator imposes its view of what is desirable. No longer is it actively promoting competition: instead, it is trying to interfere in industry decisions, including those about tariffs and, in the process, raising prices and the profits of suppliers.[13]

Ofgem's actions suggest a lack of understanding about how markets supply information and how consumers make choices when product attributes are complex. In any market where the products of different suppliers are physically the same, as in both gas and electricity, innovation and competition will concentrate on other aspects of the products such as service standards and prices. Although tariffs may proliferate and consumers may find it hard and time-consuming to make price comparisons unaided, a natural outcome is the emergence of price comparison websites, of which there are several in the energy field, which help consumers determine the best deals for them and make supplier switching straightforward. It seems patronising to assume that consumers can only make decisions if the regulator acts on their behalf to narrow their field of choice. Moreover, such actions will surely restrict innovation in tariffs, which seems a curious thing to do at a time when 'smart meters' are at last coming into use (Littlechild 2014b).

---

13 An unintended consequence of the growth of price controls and other regulatory intervention may be to increase the opportunities for capture of the regulator by the industry. Capture is unlikely to be an issue when the regulator's prime aim is to promote competition.

Proposed government retail price controls

As regards direct government price controls, as distinct from price controls by regulators, they have generally been eschewed in recent years, in energy and elsewhere. However, energy market suppliers (especially the 'Big Six') have become unpopular because they have increased prices considerably (though during a period of rising wholesale prices and expensive interventions by both government and Ofgem) and because of billing and other customer service problems. In such circumstances, there will appear to be votes in political action that curbs the activities of the energy companies, including placing restraints on the prices they can charge. It was in that context, in the autumn of 2013, that the call for energy price controls was led by Ed Miliband, leader of the Labour Party, when he promised a two-year price freeze on gas and electricity prices (apparently for both households and businesses) if Labour was elected to government. Other political leaders responded, though with different proposals: Sir John Major, former Conservative Prime Minister, called for a windfall tax on the energy suppliers and David Cameron decided to reduce some of the 'green' levies on the suppliers so as to keep prices down (Robinson 2014).

The consequences of government energy price controls

The general case against price controls was outlined at the beginning of this chapter. In general, if the controls were effective they would have demand-increasing, supply-reducing effects, leading to excess demand at the imposed price level. In the case of the UK energy market, price controls would be introduced into a market already subject to significant damaging actions by government and regulator.

The impact effect

The impact effect is uncertain because of the different ways suppliers might react. A price cap in the form of a freeze announced long in advance, as in the case of the Miliband proposal, gives suppliers an incentive to begin the freeze at as high a base as possible. Therefore, they may want to increase retail prices (or to fail to reduce them if world energy prices decline (see, for example, RWE 2014)) before the freeze takes effect. Conceivably, therefore, pre-emptive action might render an attempted freeze ineffective in the sense that prices are no lower than they would have been without it. Prices could even be higher if companies buy electricity and gas a long way ahead to avoid the effects of a freeze. Other possible pre-emptive actions include voluntary supplier price freezes,[14] perhaps in the hope of escaping political action, though any such freeze is likely to allow leeway against unexpected developments in costs and world energy prices.

The compatibility of floors and ceilings

The compatibility of a retail price cap with changes in input prices is another awkward issue which could affect the extent to which a cap is binding. If, for instance, world energy prices rose considerably, would the cap have to be specifically lifted to avoid a sharp squeeze on supplier profits? Or would there be an automatic 'pass-through' provision for input price increases? Even if world prices remain stable, a problem could arise because the government's own interventionist measures, including the carbon price floor (see below), will over the next few years raise the prices paid by energy suppliers for their inputs. Clearly, a cap on output prices does not sit easily with a (rising) floor for input

---

14   One supplier, SSE, has already announced such a freeze until 2016.

prices. It is unclear how a government which had imposed a price cap would deal with a situation in which supplier profits were being squeezed because of its own earlier measures.

The consequences of holding down prices

If we assume, despite the uncertainty about prices with and without a freeze, that prices are held below the level which would otherwise have prevailed, then, if Labour were elected, there could be some near-term shortages as demand is increased and supply falls short. Current profitability would be squeezed and, depending on expectations about future prices, there would most likely be a significant adverse effect on investment incentives, which could be serious given the circumstances of the UK energy market, where there are already concerns about the adequacy of electricity generating capacity in very cold weather conditions, caused primarily not by market forces but by government action.[15]

At the time of privatisation, fears were expressed that electricity and gas suppliers would not invest for the future once they were no longer under state control. Such fears proved unjustified, as might have been expected: companies have a strong incentive to invest if they perceive profitable investment opportunities resulting from incipient capacity shortages. The power shortages and voltage reductions common under nationalisation became rarities after privatisation. However, as explained above, in recent years government has again begun to intrude on investment decisions, particularly those concerning power stations, pressing supply companies to invest in generation from low-carbon energy sources favoured by government. The ostensible objective has been to combat future anthropogenic global warming,

---

15 See, for example, Royal Academy of Engineering (2013). Ofgem (2014) is more sanguine because it believes that the electricity market reforms now being implemented will reduce the risk of supply interruptions.

though governments have also claimed that energy security will be improved.[16]

The effect of government action to promote favoured fuels[17]

Among the measures introduced are a carbon price floor of £16 per tonne, rising to £18 per tonne in 2016 (much higher rates than under the EU Emissions Trading Scheme) in an attempt to stimulate low-carbon energy sources;[18] powers to introduce 'feed-in tariffs', under the 2013 Energy Act, with a 'contracts-for-differences' system centred on a relatively high, above-market 'strike price' intended to increase the profitability of low-carbon generators and thereby encourage them to invest; and emissions performance standards for new power stations to ensure that they keep emissions within the limits that government thinks desirable. These measures are in addition to the regime the government has operated for some years under which generators must have 'renewable obligation certificates' to show that they are installing the amounts of renewable capacity required by government. Nuclear power too is favoured, as it has been in the past: the coalition government, after long negotiations, agreed to pay EDF about twice the current price for the electricity it generates from a new nuclear station at Hinkley in Somerset for about 35 years (DECC 2013). In addition, obligations have been imposed on energy companies (the costs of which they recover in prices, thus imposing them on all consumers), intended to encourage consumers to use non-fossil sources and to cut energy use.

---

16 For a critical analysis of whether policy will achieve these objectives, see Robinson (2014)

17 More detail is in Robinson (2014).

18 The original plan was to raise the price to £30 per tonne by 2020, but in 2014 the 2016–20 price was capped at £18 per tonne.

As regards natural gas, the generating source the generators themselves would most likely have preferred, governments have blown hot and cold so that potential investors have been uncertain about the official attitude: in a politicised market, that is enough to deter investment. At the same time, the government has undertaken a 'reform' of the wholesale electricity market, which has involved protracted discussions and caused considerable uncertainty, particularly about a 'capacity mechanism', which would not have been necessary had markets been allowed to operate. Another very significant intervention has been implementation of the EU's Large Combustion Plants Directive (LCPD), designed to reduce emissions, which has resulted in the premature closure of a considerable amount of coal-fired electricity capacity (and some oil plant).

In such a politicised environment it is not surprising that, while coal and oil plant has been closing because of the LCPD, there has been little investment in new plant other than in the types favoured by government. Table 9 shows the change in

Table 9   UK electrical generating plant capacity: major power producers* (MW)

	End 2010	End 2013	Change, 2010–13
Coal	23,085	20,336	−2,749
Oil	3,638	1,370	−2,268
Mixed/dual fired	6,116	1,180	−4,936
Combined cycle gas turbines	31,724	32,967	+1,243
Nuclear	10,865	9,906	−959
Hydro	4,135	4,136	+1
Wind	1,867	3,905	+2,038
Other (including other renewables)	2,002	2,705	+703
Total	83,432	76,505	−6,927

*Maximum allowed export capacity on to transmission system. Small-scale hydro, wind and solar photovoltaics capacities are shown derated to allow for their intermittency.
Source: DECC, Digest of UK Energy Statistics 2014, Table 5.6.

generating capacity of the major UK generators from end 2010 to end 2013. Capacity at conventional steam stations (coal, oil and mixed/dual-fired) has declined by about 10,000 MW over the three years and nuclear capacity has fallen by nearly 1,000 MW. These declines have been only partly offset by a small increase of just over 1,000 MW in combined cycle gas turbines and around 3,000 MW of wind and other renewables. The reduction in total capacity has therefore been almost 7,000 MW.

There are further reductions in conventional steam plant to come because of EU directives. Between mid 2013 and end 2015 over 4,000 MW of such plant will probably be shut down and more may close thereafter under a subsequent directive (Royal Academy of Engineering 2013).

Creating uncertainty

Government and regulatory action has already created considerable uncertainty in the energy market, which has led to an environment unfavourable to new investment.[19] The threat of a retail price cap has added to this uncertainty. If the threat becomes a reality, the effect would depend on how it affected suppliers' expectations not just about prices but about government policy in general. Even if the freeze is temporary, suppliers are likely to assume that a government which had introduced one freeze might introduce another or take other comparable action. Enhanced political uncertainty would raise their cost of capital, further dampening investment and reducing supply relative to demand. Consequently, a cap might well have a perverse effect, tipping a market where suppliers are already reluctant to invest into future shortages, leading eventually to higher and not lower prices.

---

19 The effects of uncertainty, including regulatory uncertainty, on investment are analysed in Baker et al. (2013). See also www.policyuncertainty.com for measures of policy uncertainty in major economies.

Conclusions

Discussion of price capping reveals the paradoxes and inconsistencies of policy towards the energy industries. While politicians appear keen to keep down energy prices, both government and regulator have in recent years pursued policies that have increased prices and reduced competition. Government promotion of renewables and nuclear power has raised the costs of generation and Ofgem's efforts at 'simpler' and 'fairer' pricing have increased retail prices. Introducing a price cap into a managed market where the incentive to invest has already been damaged by government policy is unlikely to keep prices down, except possibly in the very short term. It is indeed more likely to give them another upward twist as well as compromising security of energy supply.

The symptoms politicians and regulators are trying to address arise from the apparent lack of competition in gas and electricity. As UK energy has reverted from a liberalised to a managed market in which competition seems weak, particularly in the domestic sector, suppliers have felt able to raise prices to households and small business (albeit at a time of rising world energy prices and government-imposed 'green' charges), confident that their 'rivals' would follow. The competitive process, so effective early this century, has been attenuated. The blame rests largely on successive governments which have tried to fix the market in favour of certain energy sources, aided by a regulator which no longer operates independently but is subservient to government.

In a recognition of this evident lack of competition in gas and electricity markets, in June 2014 an investigation by the Competition and Markets Authority was launched after a reference made by Ofgem (CMA 2014). The investigation is potentially very wide-ranging since it relates to 'the supply and acquisition of energy in Great Britain' but, as far as retail markets are concerned, it relates only to households and small business, excluding supplies to large businesses where Ofgem evidently thinks competition is effective.[20] All such competition inquiries face fundamental problems in that they tend to take a 'snapshot' view of the relevant market: it is very difficult for them to address the more pertinent question of whether or not they can perceive a competitive process which is operating over time. It will be especially difficult for the CMA to deal with a case in which the main culprits for the lack of competition appear to be the government and the energy regulator. Its investigation will find it hard to resolve the fundamental problems afflicting the energy market. What seems to be required now is simple to state but may be very difficult to implement because of the loss of face which would be involved. Instead of more and more intervention, including interference in pricing decisions by government and regulator, it would be more appropriate to reinstate a genuinely independent regulator which gives priority to promoting competition and avoids detailed meddling with prices.

References

Averch, H. A. and Johnson, L. L. (1962) Behavior of the firm under regulatory constraint. *American Economic Review* 52: 1052–69.

Baker, S., Bloom, N. and Davis, S. (2013) Measuring economic policy uncertainty. Mimeo, Stanford and Chicago.

Beesley, M. E. and Littlechild, S. C. (1983) Privatisation: principles, problems and priorities. Lloyds Bank Review, July.

Comptroller and Auditor General (2003) The new electricity trading arrangements in England and Wales. HC 624, May.

Crew, M. A. and Kleindorfer, P. R. (2006) Regulation, pricing and social welfare. In *International Handbook on Economic Regulation* (ed. M. Crew and D. Parker). Cheltenham: Edward Elgar.

20 The CMA's Statement of Issues also says that it does not intend to investigate wholesale gas markets, gas interconnection and storage and regulation of revenues from transmission and distribution (CMA 2014, paragraph 60).

DECC (2012) Energy bill provisions for Ofgem strategy and policy statement. Ref. 12D/453. www.gov.uk/government/uploads/system/uploads/attachment_data/file/65669/7202-energy-bill-provisions-for-ofgem-strategy-and-supp.pdf (accessed 11 March 2015).

DECC (2013) Initial agreement reached on new nuclear power station at Hinkley. DECC Press Release, 21 October 2013.

DTI (Department of Trade and Industry) (2007) Meeting the energy challenge: a white paper on energy (Cm 7124, May). Norwich: HMSO. http://webarchive.nationalarchives.gov.uk/20090609003228/http://www.berr.gov.uk/files/file39387.pdf (accessed 11 March 2015).

Hayek, F. A. (1948) The meaning of competition. In *Individualism and Economic Order*. London: George Routledge.

Heald, D. (1980) The economic and financial control of UK nationalised industries. *Economic Journal* 90: 243–65.

Krautkraemer, J. A. (1998) Nonrenewable resource scarcity. *Journal of Economic Literature* 36: 2065–107.

Littlechild, S. C. (2014a) Ofgem's fairer prices crusade. *City AM*, 28 June.

Littlechild, S. C. (2014b) A bureaucratic nightmare risks stifling innovation in Britain's energy market. *City AM*, 25 July.

Littlechild, S. C. (2014c) Submission to the CMA. https://assets.digital.cabinet-office.gov.uk/media/53f4abb2ed915d11d000000d/RWE_IS_response_combined.pdf (accessed 10 March 2015).

Marshall, E. (2005) Energy regulation and competition after the white paper. In *Governments, Competition and Utility Regulation* (ed. C. Robinson). Cheltenham and Northampton, MA: Edward Elgar.

Marshall, E. and Robinson, C. (1984) Gas and electricity prices. *Economic Affairs*, January 1984.

National Audit Office (1999) Giving customers a choice – the introduction of competition into the domestic gas market. HC 403, Session 1998–99, May.

Ofgem (2014) Electricity capacity assessment 2014, June. www.ofgem.gov.uk//electricity/wholesale-market/electricity-security-supply (accessed 10 March 2015).

National Audit Office (2000) Giving domestic customers a choice of electricity supplier. HC 85, Session 2000–01.

Robinson, C. (2004) Gas, electricity and the energy review. In *Successes and Failures in Regulating and Deregulating Utilities* (ed. C. Robinson). Cheltenham and Northampton, MA: Edward Elgar.

Robinson, C. (2013) Energy policy: a full circle? In *Handbook on Energy and Climate Change* (ed. R. Fouquet). Cheltenham and Northampton, MA: Edward Elgar.

Robinson, C. (2014) From nationalisation to state control: the return of centralised energy planning. IEA Discussion Paper.

Robinson, C. and Marshall, E. (2006) The regulation of energy: issues and pitfalls. In *International Handbook on Economic Regulation* (ed. M. Crew and D. Parker). Cheltenham: Edward Elgar.

Royal Academy of Engineering (2013) GB electricity capacity margin, October. http://www.raeng.org.uk/news/publications/list/reports/RAEng_GB_Electricity_capacity_margin_report.pdf (accessed 10 March 2015).

RWE npower (2014) CMA submission. https://assets.digital.cabinet-office.gov.uk/media/53f4abb2ed915d11d000000d/RWE_IS_response_combined.pdf (accessed 10 March 2015).

Seldon, A. (1990) *Capitalism*. Oxford: Blackwell.

7 REGULATION OF RAIL FARES

Richard Wellings

Introduction

Britain's railway industry was privatised in the mid 1990s. The nominal transfer of ownership to the private sector did not, however, mean an end to state control. Intervention took three key forms. Firstly, the sector remained heavily dependent on government subsidies. Indeed, the amount of taxpayer support rose significantly in real terms during the decade after privatisation, to roughly treble the levels during the 1980s. State funding for the heavy-rail network as a whole is currently running at approximately £6 billion per year, with about 40 per cent of industry spending funded by the taxpayer.[1] Secondly, the government imposed a complex artificial structure on the industry, partly in response to European Commission 'open access' rules.[2] Fragmentation was favoured over vertical integration, with separate companies owning the track and operating the trains. Finally, the government imposed strict regulations on the railways. These market interventions permeate the sector and include complex franchising rules for train operating companies and price controls on a high proportion of fares.

---

1   This figure includes non-Network Rail spending on the heavy-rail network, including Transport for London spending on the Crossrail project and London Overground. It does not include London Underground, other subway systems or light rail/tram systems. See DFT (2014a) for indicative estimates.

2   See, for example, Directive 91/440/EEC.

This chapter examines the economic impact of the latter on Britain's railways. The analysis takes into account the interaction of fare regulation with the other policies summarised above, as well as wider trends in British transport policy. The first section sets out the scope of fare regulation, examining the types of journey that are affected. The economic consequences are then analysed. In the context of the negative effects on efficiency, widely acknowledged within the industry, the government's stated rationales for price controls are assessed. It is concluded that the arguments for fare regulation are weak and that the self-interested behaviour of policymakers and rail firms explains the continued imposition of these economically damaging interventions in the transport market.

The scope of fare regulation

Regulated fares make up approximately 50 per cent of passenger revenue on the heavy-rail network. While the precise rules are complicated and intricate (see Butcher 2014), the main market segments that have been subject to price controls are as follows:

- All season tickets to, from and within London zones 1–6.
- Oyster pay-as-you-go peak and off-peak fares for journeys within London zones 1–6.
- Anytime day singles and returns for journeys to any London zones 1–6 station from a defined suburban area, roughly 35–50 miles from central London.
- Anytime day singles and returns within London.
- Off-peak, walk-up 'saver' fares for long-distance journeys (both the price and the time restrictions on these fares are regulated).
- Various weekly season tickets that are not covered by other fare regulations.
- Commuter fares and some off-peak fares in areas under the jurisdiction of Passenger Transport Executives and equivalent bodies.

Increases in these fares are limited by inflation-linked price formulae determined by central government (the vast majority of the regulated market) or the relevant regional transport agency. Before 2004, the government set regulated fares at the July Retail Prices Index (RPI) minus 1 per cent, resulting in below-inflation rises. From 2004 to 2013, the change was set by the government at July RPI plus 1 per cent. However, in December 2013, the Chancellor of the Exchequer announced that the 2014 rise would be in line with the RPI (ibid.: 3).

The economic impact of fare regulation

Economic theory suggests price ceilings lead to shortages since they encourage more demand than would occur at the market price while reducing supply. In the passenger rail market this effect is manifested in overcrowding on many of the routes on which fares are regulated, with supplied capacity insufficient to cope with the artificially inflated demand at certain times of day. More broadly, price controls can be expected to limit entrepreneurship, innovation and market segmentation in the rail industry, since, for example, the scope for offering passengers different trade-offs between price and quality of service is constrained (see Starkie 2013).

However, such analysis is complicated by the high degree of state control over the sector, with key decisions on resource allocation subject to political interference and bureaucratic central planning. Thus fare regulation should also be assessed in terms of its impact on the incentives facing the government actors who have largely supplanted commercial decision-making on the railways.

Many of the effects of price controls are already well known within the rail industry (see McNulty 2011). For example, off-peak saver fares are responsible for severe overcrowding on some services at the end of the evening peak. Instead of a gradual drop in prices as demand subsides, as would occur under market conditions, the regulation creates a cliff edge with a big fall in fare levels immediately after the departure times when saver fares become valid (typically around 7 p.m.). There is a particularly severe problem with 'artificial demand peaks' on Friday evenings on some long-distance services to the north and Scotland. Reports describe sardine-like conditions and hundreds of passengers left on the platform.[3] Fare regulation creates the perverse situation where there is often substantial spare capacity on the peak services that leave at the most convenient times, but overcrowding on less convenient services that depart later in the evening. The role of the price mechanism in allocating capacity efficiently is undermined.

A similar problem afflicts regulated commuter routes. In this case, fare regulation means that passengers travelling at the very busiest peak times typically pay the same as those commuting during the shoulders of the peak. Once again, the result is severe overcrowding on some services. Train operators are prevented from using the price mechanism to make better use of capacity by incentivising passengers to shift to quieter services. The marginal cost of each additional passenger may be very high on overcrowded trains, but regulation means fares cannot reflect this. The government recently considered introducing higher-rate 'super-peak' fares to address this problem – still a form of price control but a better approximation for market pricing. But this was rejected, apparently for political reasons (DfT 2013: 20):

> Allowing train operators to charge a premium in the 'super peak' ... would boost efficient capacity utilisation, which in the medium to longer term could help curb overall fare rises.

---

3   For example, 'Rail firms push for budget airline-style fares to beat off-peak overcrowding', *The Guardian*, 7 November 2010.

In the short-term however this would result in additional fare rises for some passengers and in the current climate with other pressures on household budgets that is not something we can accept. *We have decided against super peak pricing* as we believe it simply would not be right to impose a further burden on hard-pressed commuters at this time. We have listened to passengers... [emphasis in original]

This kind of fare regulation also tends to narrow the gap between peak and off-peak fares,[4] exacerbating overcrowding problems by reducing the financial incentives for travellers to use trains with spare capacity. Indeed, a greater difference between peak and off-peak fares would incentivise employers to shift their schedules to reduce the travel costs of their employees and customers. For example, universities could start their lectures later in the morning. By providing such incentives, market pricing delivers much more efficient use of existing capacity. This is important not just for commuters standing in packed carriages but also for taxpayers and the wider economy.

The marginal cost of a journey is particularly high when not just the train is full, but the infrastructure itself has reached capacity. The provision of new heavy-rail capacity is typically extremely expensive, as demonstrated by recent schemes such Crossrail. Moreover, the new infrastructure is typically not commercially viable, forcing taxpayers to fund a high proportion of the budgets. And price controls also make it more difficult to reclaim the costs of new infrastructure from the major beneficiaries – i.e. commuters on the busiest peak-time services – as would happen in a commercial investment, thus making subsidies from the taxpayer much more likely. Accordingly, the combination of price controls and state subsidy turns the allocation of resources

---

4   In contrast to the regulation of off-peak 'saver' fares on intercity services, which tends artificially to widen the gap immediately before and after peak periods.

on the railways into a political rather than a commercial process. Fare regulations generate problems of overcrowding which in turn put pressure on policymakers to provide additional infrastructure.

Indexation to the general inflation rate

A further problem with the current system of fare regulation is its indexation to the Retail Prices Index (RPI). There is no particular reason to expect rail industry costs to rise in line with general price inflation. The prices of goods and services within different sectors rise at different rates. For example, in recent years there have been significant price falls in sectors such as computer hardware, due to rapid innovation and the removal of trade barriers. Falling prices in these sectors will lower the RPI. Of course, this means that prices in other sectors will be rising at a faster rate than the aggregate figure. If rail industry costs were to increase faster than general inflation, but fares were pegged to RPI, government would be obliged to make up the difference at taxpayers' expense, assuming a given level of service, etc. The opposite could also occur, for example, if there were major productivity improvements on the railways, although in general this would be less objectionable since the effect would be to reduce the forced contribution of taxpayers. Nevertheless, it can be seen that the reliance of price controls on aggregate inflation indexes disrupts the market relationship between industry costs and fare levels leading to a misallocation of resources.

The rationale for fare regulation

The above discussion confirms that the well-known economic costs of price controls are pervasive in the rail sector. In this context, the government's own arguments for fare regulation deserve scrutiny. A key question is whether there are valid economic justifications for the price controls or whether their imposition reflects political considerations.

Post-privatisation controls on London commuter fares appear to have been driven by fears about the potential 'market power' of operators on these routes (SRA 2003). According to the Department for Transport (2012: 18):

> London commuters were considered to be a 'captive market' with no realistic alternative to the train for travelling into London. It was considered that this group of passengers needed to be protected against the risk of possible exploitation by train operators, who exercise a de facto monopoly position on commuting routes into London from many locations.

According to this argument, recent transport policies appear to have strengthened the case for regulation (ibid.):

> [C]ommuting into London by car has become slower and more expensive. As a result, the capital's commuters are even more captive to rail than when fares regulation was first established. So it is clear that we need to continue to use regulation to protect commuters from possible exploitation.

Arguments about 'market power' have also been used to justify regulation in the PTE areas and around other major cities. Train operators are said to operate in a semi-monopoly position leading to a presumption in favour of protecting commuters by controlling the structure and level of fares.

Even outside the travel-to-work areas of the major conurbations, a case for regulation has been made on the grounds that passengers need protection against possible exploitation by operators where they have no realistic alternative to the train. The regulation of intercity 'saver' fares widens the rationale further still (ibid.: 20):

Given the uncertainty as to how the newly privatised train operating companies would act, it was considered prudent to regulate to ensure that an affordably priced walk-up fare continued
to be available for long-distance travel during the off-peak
... This was to ensure that rail continued to offer an affordable
alternative to the private car for such trips, reflecting the wider
social benefits of leisure-related travel such as visiting family
and friends.

A critique of the case for fare regulation

The above case for price controls can be challenged on a number
of grounds. A general point is that market-power issues do not
necessarily justify state intervention. Regulation is far from costless and is prone to economic calculation problems and capture
by special interests. Thus the costs of intervention may exceed
the alleged costs of the original 'market failure' (Demsetz 1969).

In any case, the market power of rail firms would seem to be
greatly exaggerated by the government. Although sunk costs
and planning restrictions make it very difficult for new entrants
to build competing infrastructure, rail is just one element in a
diverse market for mobility that now includes low-cost virtual
options such as video-conferencing and home-working. Transport markets are therefore highly contestable and competition
would act as a check on any rail firm seeking to take advantage
of its 'market power'. This is particularly obvious outside the
London commuter belt where rail accounts for a very small proportion of journeys.[5] One might also consider the extent to which
any increase in the 'market power' of rail firms is the result of
government policies imposed since the mid 1990s, which have
deliberately discouraged competing modes such as the private
motor car (Wellings 2006). Low-cost transport modes seen in the

5   In Britain as a whole, rail accounts for only 3 per cent of trips (DfT 2014b).

developing world, such as shared taxis and private minibuses, have also effectively been prohibited in the UK.

Within Greater London itself there is clearly substantial contestability, even in the context of the state suppression of many low-cost options. Heavy rail competes with London Underground services in much of the capital. There is also an extensive bus network offering relatively cheap fares to the main employment hubs. While the congestion charge and parking fees make driving too costly for many commuters, there are other private options. A high proportion of the city's population lives within practical cycling distance of the central area, while motorbikes offer another fast and low-cost alternative. Some travellers might choose a combination of modes to make savings through competition – for example, by driving from their home to a nearby tube station, bus route or a railway operated by a different train company.

Many of the above options are also available to longer-distance commuters travelling into central London from well outside the city boundary. In addition, it should be noted that there is a large and thriving commuter coaching industry already operating in competition with the railways. Journey times are typically slower but stops may be more convenient and fares are around 40 per lower than rail (Starkie 2013: 52). Coaches also offer pre-booked seats and wi-fi, enabling passengers to work during their trip (difficult on an overcrowded train).

In the longer term, train fares will of course affect the locational decisions of households. High prices will incentivise employees to move closer to work, even if this means living in less spacious housing or a less desirable area. Alternatively, households might move to a transport corridor in which cheaper journeys are available, for example, one served by a cheaper train operating company or low-cost commuter coaches.

Finally, improvements in communications technology mean that a high proportion of commuters now have the option of working from home for at least some of the week. At the margin, higher fares would incentivise some workers to make fewer journeys. Overall there has been an 18 per cent fall in the number of commuter trips per person in England since the mid 1990s, a development which might partly be explained by such innovations (DfT 2014b).

The various alternatives available to commuters effectively lower the revenue-maximising level of fares that can be charged by train companies, and, to use the government's terminology, severely limit their 'market power'.

If the economic rationale for regulating commuter fares is weak, it is weaker still for off-peak, long-distance journeys. There is ample spare capacity on the relevant train services and operators have strong incentives to offer low-cost tickets to reflect the very low marginal cost of additional passengers. This is indeed what happened after privatisation, with very cheap pre-booked off-peak fares becoming widely available. It seems likely that in the absence of regulation, some firms would also have offered low-cost tickets bought at stations immediately prior to travel or even on the train, albeit on a more restricted range of services.

Furthermore, the market for intercity travel is clearly highly contestable, with a very high rate of car ownership among the socio-economic groups who most frequently make such journeys. Extensive route networks are operated by coach firms such as National Express and Megabus, which offer fares as low as £1.50 for long-distance trips,[6] while many routes are also served by airlines. In addition, there is competition between rail firms on many routes. For example, a passenger travelling from London to Birmingham could choose Virgin Trains, Chiltern Railways or London Midland services. Yorkshire can be reached using East Coast, East Midlands Trains, Grand Central or Hull Trains. Modal combinations further increase the choice available to

6   See https://www.megabus.com/.

travellers, for instance, by enabling them to drive part of a journey then take the remainder by train.

Incentives for fare regulation

Given the contestability of transport markets, even in the London commuter market but particularly on long-distance intercity journeys, an analysis of fare regulation should also examine alternative explanations for the imposition of price controls. A plausible hypothesis is that regulation has been driven primarily by the self-interest of key actors in the development of rail policy.

In the early 1990s rail privatisation was deeply unpopular and faced strong opposition among backbench Conservative MPs. There were fears that steep fare hikes could result in the loss of marginal constituencies, particularly in the London commuter belt, where rail commands a significant market share.

Accordingly, fare regulation may be better understood as a political policy rather than an economic one. It was arguably designed to counter opponents' claims that privatisation would negatively affect the lives of key voting groups and fears it would deepen the unpopularity of an already weak government. Price controls were just one element of this risk-averse policy agenda, which also, for example, imposed regulations that made it very difficult for the industry to close even the most heavily loss-making lines.

Wolmar (2001: 68) quotes one senior British Rail official:

> I came across a number of confidential privatisation papers circulating about fare levels ... These, when leaked (and they all implied fare rises and a loss of multi-operator tickets), were, I think, instrumental in forcing the Tory government to regulate real fares downward, reversing the trend they had applied to BR.

He continues (ibid.: 68–69):

[F]ares regulation was one of the great victories for opponents of the privatisation. The original plan had been to regulate fares only where train operators had a virtual monopoly – such as on the London commuter routes ... but ministers were keen to make privatisation more palatable and eventually, late in the process, a scheme to regulate season tickets, savers and some other fares was implemented as a sop to passengers. It was a marked reversal from BR's policy of using fares to restrict growth but, as with all aspects of privatisation, the implications for the economics of the railway were not thought through.

A rent-seeking coalition against taxpayers

Arguably the decision to introduce and persist with these policies has not just been the result of politicians seeking to 'buy votes'. After privatisation, the range of special interest groups with a stake in the rail industry – and hence government subsidies – expanded significantly to include various commercial entities such as train operating companies, lawyers, consultants and banks. As public choice theory explains, small, concentrated interest groups have far stronger incentives to devote resources to influencing policy than dispersed groups such as taxpayers. They also face fewer organisational problems and can more easily prevent free-riding (Olson 1965).

While fare regulation is a source of significant inefficiencies in the rail sector, various special interests benefit from its existence and the resulting market distortions. Clearly, subsets of passengers perceive benefits from the arrangement, to the extent that it reduces their travel costs. Yet costs are imposed on those passengers who would prefer to pay higher fares in order to avoid overcrowding and associated delays. And travellers are inevitably ignorant of the potential benefits from the entrepreneurship, innovation and market segmentation that are hindered by the regulations.

The rail industry itself is a major beneficiary. Price controls increase demand, particularly during peak periods, creating artificial capacity problems that are eventually 'solved' by large-scale state spending on railway infrastructure and new rolling stock. Such taxpayer support provides substantial financial gains to interests such as Network Rail officials, DfT bureaucrats, various consultancies, engineering firms and train manufacturers.

Thus it may be hypothesised that fare regulation and the resulting disbursement of state funds sustains a 'distributional coalition' of special interests who gain financially from the current regulatory system. According to Olson (1982: 44), distributional coalitions are 'overwhelmingly oriented to struggles over the distribution of income and wealth rather than to the production of additional output'. In other words they are engaged in 'rent-seeking' behaviour, extracting resources from the wider population through preferential subsidies and regulation. Such a group has 'little or no incentive to make any significant sacrifices in the interest of the society; it can best serve its members' interests by striving to seize a large share of society's production for them. This will be expedient, moreover, even if the social costs of the change in the distribution exceed the amount redistributed by a huge multiple' (ibid.).

While a detailed analysis is beyond the scope of this paper, it is clear that the rail industry commits substantial resources to rent-seeking activities. For example, lobbying for the High Speed 2 rail project has been undertaken by special interests such as engineering firms, train manufacturers and transport bureaucracies (see Wellings 2013). Claims that the southern West Coast Main Line – which carries, among other traffic, regulated-fare commuter services – will soon be full, have been central to the public relations campaign for the new line. Proponents ignore the potential for more flexible pricing and market segmentation to make more intensive use of existing infrastructure.

Similarly, price controls have successfully been promoted through the Fair Fares Now campaign run by the Campaign for Better Transport, which calls for 'cheaper – affordable rail fares, including peak times and turn-up-and-go tickets', regulated fares to 'fall gradually, over time to the European average' and for the 'high premium paid for flexibility and peak-time travel' to be reduced.[7] Such policies are clearly a recipe for higher subsidies from the taxpayer and would benefit significantly the distributional coalition represented by the rail lobby. And while the connection between the funding of organisations and their campaigning activity is not always clear cut, it is nevertheless the case that the Campaign for Better Transport is supported financially by major players in the sector. In the post-privatisation era, supporters have included several train operating companies, as well as various government agencies.[8]

Another influential organisation, Passenger Focus, which has campaigned in support of fare regulation and opposed more flexibility in pricing, is sponsored directly by the Department of Transport (DfT), ostensibly in order to represent the interests of passengers. In 2013–14, the organisation received £4,930,000 'grant in aid' from the DfT (Passenger Focus 2014: 15). Thus the government is effectively using taxpayers' money to lobby itself (Snowdon 2012). Government officials employed to direct the rail industry are of course an important component of the distributional coalition.

However, it should be pointed out that there are constraints on such redistribution, for example in terms of the overall level of public spending and debt, as well as the voting power of taxpayers. While the incentives for the latter to engage in debates on the level of rail subsidy are very weak indeed, they may exhibit

---

7   http://www.bettertransport.org.uk/fair-fares-now (accessed 10 March 2015).

8   See Campaign for Better Transport Charitable Trust Report and Financial Statements, various years, and Transport 2000 Annual Review, various years.

dissatisfaction with the overall level of taxation. And the rail lobby has to compete with numerous other distributional coalitions for state funds. Within government, HM Treasury constrains the budgets of state bureaucracies, including the various transport agencies.

Phasing out price controls

Fare regulation is partly responsible for the major problems facing Britain's railways. It distorts patterns of demand, leading to overcrowding on some routes at certain times of day, while at the same time hindering use of the price mechanism to make better use of existing capacity. In turn, these inefficiencies create political pressure for the government to fund expensive infrastructure enhancements. Price controls have thus played an important role in sustaining high levels of taxpayer support for the sector and the misallocation of investment towards poor-value rail schemes.

There is therefore a strong economic case for phasing out fare regulation completely or, at the very least, giving train operating companies far more flexibility in pricing. In particular, the introduction of 'super-peak' fares that charged passengers more for travelling during the very busiest periods, would flatten peak demand, thereby addressing overcrowding problems at low cost. Greater fare flexibility would also create possibilities for greater market segmentation, for example, by allowing train operators to introduce cut-price, high-capacity carriages (Starkie 2013: 48–52). And deregulation would enable rail firms to make infrastructure enhancements on a commercial basis, since they would be free to charge passengers higher fares for an improved service. Accordingly, the level of taxpayer subsidy could be lowered substantially with beneficial effects for the wider economy.

Phasing out price controls therefore has the potential to reduce significantly the dependence of the rail industry on government support and perhaps to remove it entirely on some parts of the network.[9] This would change dramatically the incentive structures facing the firms in the sector. Their profits would depend to a far greater extent on the services they offered to their customers. The absence of subsidies would reduce the returns from rent-seeking behaviour.[10] Thus the removal of fare regulation has the potential to break up the distributional coalition that extracts resources from taxpayers and the wider economy.

Yet key elements of this coalition would potentially suffer substantial losses from such a policy shift, in particular, those firms and officials involved in the planning and construction of state-funded infrastructure enhancements. And, as happened during the privatisation process, reform could be obstructed by risk-averse politicians fearful of losing support from certain segments of the passenger population. In this respect it is telling that ministers recently decided to reject proposals for more flexible pricing.[11] Although the economic case for deregulating fares is very strong indeed, significant reform is unlikely while special interests continue to have a disproportionate influence over rail policy.

References

Butcher, L. (2014) *Railways: Fares*. Standard Note SN1904. London: House of Commons Library.

Demsetz, H. (1969) Information and efficiency, another viewpoint. *Journal of Law and Economics* 12(1): 1–21.

---

9   There is also a strong economic case for phasing out state subsidies on routes that would not be commercially viable, even if this resulted in line closures, although that discussion is not the focus of this paper.

10 Although lobbying for taxpayer subsidies is only one aspect of rent-seeking behaviour in the rail sector. Other targeted policy areas include regulation and industry structure (e.g. franchising arrangements).

11 See, for example, the rail minister's evidence to the Transport Select Committee, 24 April 2013. http://www.publications.parliament.uk/pa/cm201213/cmselect/cm tran/uc874-iii/uc87401.htm (accessed 10 March 2015).

DfT (Department for Transport) (2012) *Rail Fares and Ticketing Review: Initial Consultation*. London: DfT.

DfT (Department for Transport) (2013) *Rail Fares and Ticketing Review: Next Steps*. London: DfT.

DfT (Department of Transport) (2014a) *Rail Trends Great Britain 2013/14*. London: Department for Transport Rail Executive.

DfT (Department of Transport) (2014b) *National Travel Survey: England 2013*. London: DfT.

McNulty, R. (2011) *Realising the Potential of GB Rail: Report of the Rail Value for Money Study*. London: DfT/ORR.

Olson, M. (1965) *The Logic of Collective Action: Public Goods and the Theory of Groups*. Cambridge, MA: Harvard University Press.

Olson, M. (1982) *The Rise and Decline of Nations: Economic Growth, Stagflation and Social Rigidities*. New Haven, CT: Yale University Press.

Passenger Focus (2014) *Annual Report and Accounts, 2013–14*. London: HMSO.

Snowdon, C. (2012) *Sock Puppets: How the Government Lobbies Itself and Why*. London: Institute of Economic Affairs.

SRA (Strategic Rail Authority) (2003) *Fares Review Conclusions 2003 Britain's Railway, Properly Delivered*. London: SRA.

Starkie, D. (2013) *Transport Infrastructure: Adding Value*. London: Institute of Economic Affairs.

Wellings, R. (2006) Environmentalism, public choice and the railways. In *The Railways, the Market and the Government* (ed. J. Hibbs, O. Knipping, R. Merket, C. Nash, R. Roy, D. Tyrrall and R. Wellings). London: Institute of Economic Affairs.

Wellings, R. (2013) *The High-Speed Gravy Train: Special Interests, Transport Policy and Government Spending*. London: Institute of Economic Affairs.

Wolmar, C. (2001) *Broken Rails: How Privatisation Wrecked Britain's Railways*. London: Aurum Press.

8 PRICE CEILINGS IN FINANCIAL MARKETS

Philip Booth and Stephen Davies

Controls and ceilings on the quantity and cost of credit are probably the oldest form of price control. They are also among the most damaging. Often, as in the Islamic world or classical Greece, the very idea of lending money with interest attached is condemned as unnatural or impious. This was also, of course, the position of early Christians. However, so great is the need for credit in any functioning economy beyond subsistence level that, in practice, lending at interest still happens no matter what the theologians and philosophers may argue. What tends to happen, as with the medieval anti-usury laws, is that a ban on 'excessive' interest substitutes for a ban on all interest. In other words, there is a ceiling set on the level of interest that may be charged for a loan. This is quite simply a price cap and, like all such caps, it has economically damaging and disruptive effects.

Moreover, because of the central role of money in exchange and in economic activity in general, and given the central place of credit in facilitating growth and innovation, price ceilings on credit have impacts that are more extensive and harmful than those imposed on other aspects of economic life. In particular, because for every debtor there is also a creditor, interest rate caps have far reaching impacts on investment returns in general. As well as being a limit on charges to borrowers, they necessarily limit returns to certain kinds of investment and, indirectly, some or most kinds of savings.

The most common form of interest ceiling is a cap on the level or amount of interest that can be charged to a borrower. Sometimes, limitations of this kind are imposed in general, on all kinds of loans and credit and on all borrowers, as for example during the Middle Ages in Europe (at least in theory). More often, caps are imposed on specific kinds of loan or credit. In these cases the restrictions are typically applied to credit products that are disproportionately used – or thought to be used – by people on low or irregular incomes. The usual goal of a ceiling on interest is to protect borrowers on low incomes from the consequences of their own lack of financial literacy (i.e. an information asymmetry). However, this intention is usually portrayed as being a matter of protecting low-income borrowers against so-called 'predatory' lenders.

The first part of this chapter will examine interest rate caps, which are being reintroduced in Britain. The second part will examine caps on charges for other financial products, specifically caps on pension charges, which are also being introduced in the UK. Though pensions are not widely studied by finance academics and often attract little public interest, pension fund assets total around 140 per cent of national income in the UK. Thus this new policy is of considerable importance.

Interest ceilings in post-war Britain

Historically, limits on credit in the UK, including price ceilings, were primarily a tool of macroeconomic management. The goal of these was, in fact, different from the goals of the interest controls described in the introduction: it was to reduce effective aggregate demand by restricting access to credit. The most common form these controls took was a restriction on the total quantity of lending by financial institutions relative to the amount they had lent at an earlier date. As Table 10 shows, controls of this kind were imposed regularly between 1961 and the early 1970s.

Table 10   Lending ceilings as a per cent of existing lending levels in post-war Britain

Date	Description of control		
	Clearing banks	Other banks	Larger finance houses
July 1961	100% of June 1961 level	100% of June 1961 level	100% of June 1961 level
October 1962	Ceiling removed	Ceiling removed	Ceiling removed
May 1965	105% of March 1965 level	105% of March 1965 level	105% of March 1965 level
April 1967	Ceiling removed	No change	No change
November 1967	100% of November 1967 level	100% of November 1967 level	100% of October 1967 level
May 1968	104% of November 1967 level	104% of November 1967 level	No change
November 1968	98% of November 1967 level	102% of November 1967 level	98% of October 1967 level
April 1970	105% of March 1970 level	107% of March 1970 level	105% of March 1970 level
March 1971	107.5% of March 1970 level	109.5% of March 1970 level	107.5% of March 1970 level

Chancellors also imposed and removed stringent restrictions on the availability and scope of hire purchase. At the same time, Chancellors used direct controls and pressure via the Bank of England to limit the upward movement of interest rates in response to a reduction in the supply of credit relative to the demand for it. In other words, the price control was imposed to try to mitigate the consequences of a directly engineered shortage of supply by government. This attempt to control credit and interest rates was all in the context of extensive private regulation in the shape of a cartel among clearing banks and another among building societies in which these institutions did not compete with one another over deposit charges and interest rates.

One result was a lack of innovation in financial services, although this began to change towards the end of the 1960s. The main effect of the controls was a shortage of credit. The shortage could often be dramatic – mortgage 'famines' such as the one that occurred at the end of the 1970s were a recurring phenomenon.

In 1971 many of the controls on credit expansion were removed, with the aim of increasing competition in the banking sector (although building societies were unaffected). At the same time, interest rates were still kept low. The result was a sharp expansion in credit with bank lending to the private sector increasing by 33 per cent in 1973. One response was the so-called 'corset' or Supplementary Special Deposits Scheme, which forced banks to place extra non-interest-bearing deposits with the Bank of England – this was imposed three times between 1973 and 1979. However, just as a real-life corset leads to a sudden expansion of pent up flesh when removed, so each episode of this scheme was followed by a sudden surge in lending.

After the 1979 election there was a general move away from caps on credit that had been such a major feature of post-war policy. Governments of both parties encouraged innovation in the financial services sector relying on interest rates set by the central bank as the main instrument for controlling credit demand and supply. In other words, explicit controls on the price of credit were abandoned.

The reforms of the 1980s and 1990s led to a great expansion of existing kinds of credit and credit-issuing institutions. At the same time there was a great deal of product innovation and the market became much more competitive and innovative. The cartels and private agreements that had regulated most consumer credit before the late 1980s were swept away and it became much easier for new players to enter the market. The Financial Conduct Authority now estimates that there are no fewer than 50,000 firms that come under its remit and firms both enter and leave the market with far greater frequency than in the past.[1]

---

1   http://www.fca.org.uk/firms/firm-types (accessed 10 March 2015).

Interest caps on pay-day lending

One area where innovation was most dramatic was in the market for short-term credit or pay-day loans. Short-term credit has been a staple feature of British life for a long time. The best known form was pawnbroking, where short-term credit was secured against an asset (the 'pledge') that was deposited with the pawnbroker and forfeited if the loan was not repaid. Unsecured short-term credit by contrast was typically provided informally by money lenders. Since 2000, and especially since 2006, there has been rapid growth in the use of this kind of unsecured credit. There has also been significant innovation in this area and it is now offered by firms with established business structures using online application and credit checking, which speeds up the process, provides greater anonymity and can be combined with direct deposit of the loan into the applicant's bank account. All of this has made this kind of credit much more attractive to borrowers. It is this form of credit that has led to proposals for interest rate caps for the first time in the UK since the early 1980s. It is also subject to price control in other countries.

The purposes of short-term credit

Short-term credit has two main purposes. The first is to provide a way of dealing with a cash-flow problem where there are short-term demands for money that are due before anticipated income will arrive. The second, more controversial, use is to provide repeated short-term supplements to income for people who either have erratic incomes or who have 'lumpy' expenditure that does not match up smoothly with their income flow and who also do not have enough savings to deal with this problem. Short-term credit should not be used to finance purchases or pay other debts – other forms of finance are more appropriate in those cases.

Short-term lenders of unsecured credit are therefore meeting a genuine need and the kinds of innovations that have been seen since the 1990s are ones that help to fit the product more closely to consumers' desires. However, they have attracted a great deal of hostility and this has led to a move to cap the cost of this type of credit. Some of the complaints against short-term lenders relate to straightforward bad business practice, such as wrongfully sending out letters to customers that claimed to be legal demands for repayment when in fact they were not. These kinds of action should be the subject of other forms of law or regulation and, in any case, have no bearing on the nature of the product per se or its cost.

However, many of the complaints do not relate to such matters. One common subject of complaint is the annual percentage rate,[2] known as the APR, of short-term credit, which is often calculated at being well over 1,000 per cent. However, this is a misleading measure of the cost of the loan, because the term of the loan is both short and fixed and the charge attached to the loan is more in the nature of a fee for service. So a charge of £20 for a £100 two-week loan would be translated into an extremely high APR, but much of that charge will relate to the set-up costs of the loan as well as compensation for the risk of non-repayment. It is unreasonable to compound and annualise such charges. Comparing the APR from a consumer credit product with the interest rate on long-term loans is like comparing the cost of a hotel with that of renting a house and working out that the hotel is much more expensive by multiplying the nightly rate by 365 – the point is that hotels and permanent or long-stay residences are completely different products.

Another charge against the lenders is that the bulk of the profit made by companies in this sector comes from people who are unable to repay their loans on time and who roll them over,

---

2   Technically, approximate to the effective annualised rate of interest on the product.

incurring repeated charges and very high repayment costs. Certainly, a high proportion of people who take out short-term credit do indeed roll it over. However, the charge rate for outright default is no higher for this kind of credit than for others – in the US it runs at 3.2 per cent of total receivable payments for a typical lender.[3] This is because most borrowers do not actually roll over the loan repeatedly and the rollover figures are a product of the very short terms of the typical advance – in other words, the borrower wished to borrow for two or three months initially and does so by rolling over a one-month loan. At the end of the two or three months, most borrowers repay in full. What is found is that many customers use short-term credit repeatedly rather than roll over a single loan – in the UK the average customer takes out credit of this kind six times in a year (the historical usage of pawnbrokers in British working-class communities also shows this pattern). Ultimately, this is as a result of a combination of low wages (reflecting low productivity) and artificially high living costs, particularly for energy and housing.[4] Short-term credit is enabling people to deal with this situation, which would otherwise have much more serious consequences such as defaults on utility bills and mortgages or rent.

At the same time, a large number of people who take out consumer credit loans are not on low incomes. A Competition and Markets Authority survey found, for example, that: three in ten pay-day loan customers have an average annual income of more than £36,000; more than half could have used an alternative form of credit; pay-day loan customers are more likely to be in work than the population as a whole; and pay-day loan customers have similar levels of education as the population as a whole.

---

3   See page 5 of http://www.sec.gov/Archives/edgar/data/1299704/000104746912002758/a2208026z10-k.htm. (accessed 10 March 2015).

4   http://www.r3.org.uk/index.cfm?page=1114&element=19650 (accessed 10 March 2015).

Such people will generally be using consumer credit pragmatically and are not necessarily especially vulnerable.[5]

Proposed price controls in UK consumer credit markets

From 2010 onwards, political pressure grew for controls to be imposed on this type of credit, particularly price controls in the form of caps on interest charges and the total amount repayable. Following an Office of Fair Trading (OFT) report and pressure from organisations such as Compass and an early day motion in the House of Commons, the newly formed Financial Conduct Authority (FCA) announced in July 2014 that it would impose caps of this kind with effect from January 2015.[6] This decision was confirmed on 11 November 2014. Rather than setting a cap on the APR (the model used in Australia), the FCA has decreed that, for new loans, and for loans that are rolled over, interest and fees combined must not exceed 0.8 per cent per day of the amount borrowed while default fees are capped at £15 for any one loan. The total cost of a loan must not exceed the actual amount borrowed (so if £100 is borrowed, the lender cannot require repayment of more than £200). All of this is in addition to other kinds of regulation already announced such as limits on the number of allowed rollovers, which will themselves raise business costs and reduce profit margins significantly.[7]

The FCA argues in its preliminary paper that it has considered various options and has rejected calls for a cap at a level that would make almost all lending of this kind uneconomic.

---

5   https://assets.digital.cabinet-office.gov.uk/media/5329df8aed915d0e5d000339/14 0131_payday_lending_tns_survey_report_.pdf (accessed 10 March 2015).

6   For the initial consultation paper, see http://www.fca.org.uk/news/cp13-10-consu mer-credit-detailed-proposals (accessed 10 March 2015). The final proposals are at http://www.fca.org.uk/news/cp14-10-proposals-for-a-price-cap-on-high-cost-sh ort-term-credit (accessed 10 March 2015).

7   http://www.bbc.com/news/business-28305886 (accessed 10 March 2015).

However, it also estimates that the caps it has imposed will reduce the revenue of the 200 firms in this area by £420 million (42 per cent).[8] This will inevitably have a dramatic effect. In fact, the FCA itself states that, in the five months between February and July of 2014 (in anticipation of the initial announcement), the number of loans and the amount borrowed fell by 35 per cent.

The impact of charge caps

The most obvious impact of charge caps is that firms will withdraw from the market and that access to short-term credit will be reduced. The remaining lenders may then tighten their requirements so as to reduce their exposure – in other words, if costs are capped, margins will be maintained by only serving the better credit risks. The FCA said in November that it expected 99 per cent of the firms operating in the sector to go out of business entirely or withdraw from this type of lending.[9] The result will be, as was the case in the 1960s and 1970s, a credit shortage for certain classes of borrower. Again, the FCA itself estimates that between 7 per cent and 11 per cent of existing borrowers will be unable to gain short-term credit in the future (some 70,000 people).[10] This is, of course, only an estimate and the methodology used means that any departure from this figure is likely to be in the direction of higher numbers rather than lower.

A common argument is that consumer credit interest caps will lead to an increase in outright illegal money lending by seriously unsavoury people who are unlikely to bother with

---

8   This and other details can be found in the full text of the consultation paper at http://www.fca.org.uk/your-fca/documents/consultation-papers/cp14-10 (accessed 10 March 2015).

9   http://www.bloomberg.com/news/2014-11-11/u-k-s-fca-to-introduce-2015-price-cap-on-payday-lenders.html (accessed 10 March 2015).

10 http://www.fca.org.uk/news/fca-confirms-price-cap-rules-for-payday-lenders (accessed 10 March 2015).

even the pretence of legal action to recover bad debts. However, evidence from the US is that, while this does happen, it is a less significant consequence than one might expect (see Mayer 2012). It is more probable that people will turn to informal social networks or family to fund their needs. This means, though, that people who are in stable social or familial networks will be less severely affected while the bulk of the impact will be felt by the vulnerable and socially isolated. Moreover, people are unlikely to be able to use connections of this kind for regular or repeated access to short-term credit. Given that most users of pay-day loans are employed, this means that problems caused by the combination of low pay and high living costs are likely to become more frequent and acute. The most likely effects down the line will be higher rates of default on items such as rent or energy bills and potentially poorer credit records for the least well off, making it more difficult for them to obtain cheap credit in the future.[11]

Another effect of this cap is that, in addition to reducing both the number of firms and the overall amount of credit being supplied, it will remove much of the incentive to innovate because it will reduce the likelihood of new entrants to the market pioneering novel practices such as online applications and evaluations. Instead, it will consolidate the position of larger players and leave them less vulnerable to challenge. The most likely outcome is an oligopolistic market – the FCA anticipates that there will be about four large lenders left.

In general, as well as reducing the total amount of credit available, there will be a reduction in the range of products. In particular, the move that was already taking place towards longer terms for loans (that would deal with the problem of missed payments and rollovers identified earlier) will almost certainly

---

11 https://assets.digital.cabinet-office.gov.uk/media/5329df8aed915d0e5d000339/14 0131_payday_lending_tns_survey_report_.pdf (accessed 10 March 2015).

be cut short by the limitation of default charges to a flat rate of £15 per loan. In other kinds of credit that have more than one payment due (such as credit cards) the usual practice is to have a non-payment fee for each instance of a missed payment and this is a more accurate reflection of business costs.

The concern about the impact of charge caps is not simply speculative. The evidence suggests that charge caps on consumer credit have significant economic and social detriment. A report for the then Department of Trade and Industry (Policis 2004) found that, in France and Germany, which both have interest rate caps, between 20 and 25 per cent of people who had trouble with debts experienced complete financial breakdown compared with 4 per cent in the UK. Financial breakdown of this kind is often accompanied by subsequent difficulties in obtaining housing, employment and the purchase of essentials such as food. Furthermore, the proportion of those who are credit impaired and who use illegal loans was reported to be tiny in the UK – around 3 per cent – while it was around 10 per cent in Germany. Those who cannot get credit, in markets where there are interest rate caps, tend to turn to even more expensive or less desirable sources of finance. These may incur much higher explicit charges or may involve the use of mail order to purchase essentials at much higher prices. Morgan and Strain (2008) in a study for the Federal Reserve Bank of New York found very undesirable effects from consumer credit restrictions (of a much more draconian type than those proposed in the UK) in some US states. They conclude (page 26):

> Georgians and North Carolinians do not seem better off since their states outlawed payday credit: they have bounced more checks, complained more about lenders and debt collectors, and have filed for Chapter 7 ('no asset') bankruptcy at a higher rate. The increase in bounced checks represents a potentially huge transfer from depositors to banks and credit unions. Banning

payday loans did not save Georgian households $154 million per year ... it cost them millions per year in returned check fees ... [Our findings are] consistent with the ... hypothesis that payday credit is cheaper than the bounce 'protection' that earns millions for credit unions and banks. Forcing households to replace costly credit with even costlier credit is bound to make them worse off.

The most serious feature of the FCA's paper, however, is their explicit statement that they are considering extending these kinds of price ceilings to other kinds of personal credit such as credit cards and unsecured loans. Indeed, it is interesting to note that short-term consumer credit products can often be better value than temporary bank overdrafts. There is a real danger that price controls on one form of credit that is currently unpopular with a political elite which seldom uses it will lead to a more widespread adoption of price ceilings on credit in general.

Charge caps on pensions

In the last year or so, politicians have been involved in a 'bidding war' to cap the cost of pension fund management. Despite UK pensions minister Steve Webb saying in 2013 that he would not cap charges,[12] while arguing that to do so would be like capping the price of a tin of baked beans, he changed his mind in 2014. Webb launched a consultation on widespread charge caps before deciding upon a cap of 0.75 per cent of funds under management for pensions built up under the auto-enrolment scheme.[13] It is

---

12 http://www.thisismoney.co.uk/money/pensions/article-2267536/Steve-Webb-Cap ping-pension-charges-like-capping-price-baked-beans.html (accessed 10 March 2015).

13 This is a special pensions sub-market, which is likely to grow rapidly over time. It relates to pensions accumulated under an arrangement whereby people are assumed to be members of a particular type of defined contribution pension scheme unless they actively opt out.

government policy to review this charge cap in 2017 and, potentially, to include other costs of pension fund management within
the cap.[14] Very shortly after Webb's announcement, the opposition Labour Party responded by promising that an initial 0.75
per cent cap would be reduced to 0.5 per cent in the course of a
parliament.[15] It is worth noting in passing that proposed charge
caps are always set at round numbers, which suggests that they
are driven by the need for politicians to obtain headlines rather
than by some attempt at determining a charge cap at which the
costs of the cap may be less than the benefits.

Market prices or politicians' preferences?

There are obvious dangers in having the price of any product
determined by politicians rather than by the market process.
Politicians may believe that they act as independent arbiters in
the public interest but the bidding war in relation to pension
charge caps suggests otherwise. To begin with, politicians or
regulators cannot know what the 'correct' level of charges should
be. Secondly, politicians and others in the political process are
not disinterested. They may well act in their own interests rather
than in the general public interest. This, in turn, may reflect the
positioning by rent-seeking interest groups within the political
process (see Tullock (2006) for a discussion of rent seeking).

One such interest group is incumbent providers of pensions. A
charge cap can reduce the threat from new entrants to the market
who could have developed more innovative products with charging structures that contravene the charge cap. For example, when
Steve Webb's initial proposal for a 0.75 per cent charge cap was
announced, Legal and General, one of the biggest incumbent insurers in the market argued that the cap was too high and should

---

14 http://www.moneymarketing.co.uk/news-and-analysis/pensions/govt-to-cap-pen
    sion-charges-at-075-from-april-2015/2008491.article (accessed 10 March 2015).

15 http://www.bbc.co.uk/news/business-26086488 (accessed 10 March 2015).

be reduced to 0.5 per cent.[16] Phil Loney, Chief Executive of a much smaller and mutual company, Royal London, noted that, after the announcement of the 0.75 per cent charge cap proposal, there was no fall in the share price of larger insurance companies and that the proposed ceiling would become a norm (in effect, both a floor and a ceiling) when the process of competition could have led to lower charges in the long term in the absence of a cap.[17]

Charge caps also lead to redistribution between different types of pension scheme members. Given that it is generally not more expensive to manage larger than smaller funds, a cap set at a given percentage of the value of a pension fund will tend to benefit savers with smaller funds. Thus, savers with smaller funds become another potential rent-seeking group in the political process.

Although there is evidence that large firms and trade bodies regularly meet government,[18] there is no clear evidence of large-scale lobbying in relation to (or indeed significant interest in) this issue. What would appear to be more plausible is that politicians are responding to what are sometimes termed 'expressive interests'. These constitute ill-informed or irrational general views along the lines suggested by, for example, Caplan (2007).[19] If the vast majority of the population is ignorant of the impact of regulation on charges, then politicians may get applause from expressive interests by appealing to people who believe they may benefit from a charge cap but who do not fully understand the implications. The general public may well believe that there are benefits from simplicity which a uniform capped charge will bring without being aware of the more subtle problems to which

---

16 http://www.bbc.co.uk/news/business-25132782 (accessed 10 March 2015).

17 http://www.moneymarketing.co.uk/opinion/phil-loney-steve-webbs-pension-cha rge-cap-is-bad-economics/2008826.article (accessed 10 March 2015).

18 http://www.moneymarketing.co.uk/2013436.article (accessed 10 March 2015).

19 The phrase 'expressive interests' was originally used by Brennan and Lomasky (1993).

it may give rise. Indeed, strong consumer support for simple charging structures has been demonstrated in energy markets (see Ofgem 2011). The benefit of market competition which leads to differentiated products with different pricing structures may not be something that consumers welcome in the abstract – and is something that the industry may well oppose too if competition can be restricted by a uniform, regulated charging structure.

This response to voters would certainly explain the fact that, as soon as the possibility of charge caps was announced, there was a 'bidding war' between the government and opposition to design 'harsher' measures. This culminated in pensions minister Steve Webb saying: 'We are going to put charges in a vice – and we will tighten the pressure year after year.'[20]

There are therefore clear disadvantages of using the political process to determine charges. The outcome may be irrational, or it may involve politicians responding to the interests of rent seekers, or both. There is also a danger that, once a regulatory role is established in this field, there are few constraints on its expansion. For example, soon after the announcement regarding pension fund charge caps, the government announced that it would also ban charges for advice and the provision of special discounts to active members still contributing to their pension funds.[21] It seems likely that the whole structure of prices in this market will become controlled by the political process responding to rent-seeking and expressive interests.

Problems caused by charge caps in fund management

(a) *Price stickiness.* Proponents of price regulation (for example, of minimum wages) often point to price stickiness within markets

---

20 http://www.independent.co.uk/news/business/news/insurers-warn-over-govern
    ment-cap-on-pension-plan-charges-9220147.html (accessed 10 March 2015).

21 Ibid.

for a justification for intervention. This is a well-known theoretical feature of oligopolistic markets covered in standard textbooks, though it is a difficult feature to investigate empirically. Oligopolists may fear that, if they raise prices, others will not follow and, given the intense competition between a few big players, demand will be elastic. On the other hand, if they lower prices, other firms may well follow and thus demand will be inelastic when an individual firm moves prices in a downward direction. Individual firms may always lose from moving prices from current levels in either direction: this can lead to price stickiness.

As noted above, it is possible for large incumbents in the pension management market to operate at a level of costs below the forthcoming charge cap. Imposing a ceiling on charges may institutionalise that level of charges and make it even less likely that a large firm in an oligopolistic market will reduce charges. A charge ceiling could exacerbate the very problem it is designed to solve and certainly provides no further incentive for incumbents to move their charges below the cap. This is not just theoretical nit picking from opponents of charge caps; the government's Office of Fair Trading itself said: 'Set too high, a cap can become a target for providers' (OFT 2014: 26).

(b) *Charge caps and market entry.* As noted, a charge cap may prevent new entry into the market and it is often new entrants that transform markets and bring hugely increased benefits for customers from innovation. Given the benefits of scale in fund management and the cost of raising capital for new entrants, it is difficult for a new entrant to compete directly with incumbents. New entrants will often have to compete on the basis of their novel features such as providing 'ethical' investments, fund management strategies that change with a member's age, bespoke services, and so on. In the first few years, new entrants may then not be able to set charges within a cap. A permanent oligopoly characterised by an absence of innovation may result. Again, as some respondents to the OFT consultation stated (Department for Work and Pensions 2014: 45): 'Furthermore, a default fund charge cap may act as an entry barrier to new providers, which, combined with the possible withdrawal of some providers, may result in an oligopoly', and 'we do see issues for the DC market if a cap is introduced at a level that could act as a barrier to entry. The DWP should ensure that the cap that is introduced does not promote imperfect competition by introducing barriers to entry'. Once again, the problem with a charge cap is that politicians do not know what the 'right' level of charge should be and, if they did know it, they would have few incentives to set the cap at that level.

(c) *Charge caps and withdrawal from the market.* A charge cap, defined as a percentage of funds under management, may well make selling business to low-paid people or people who otherwise have small savings unprofitable, leaving these markets unserved. Furthermore, the cost of administering a new contribution that is made to a fund is greater than the cost of managing money that has previously been invested. This may lead to pension providers targeting only those customers who will make the largest contributions or who make contributions for a long period of time (probably younger-to-middle-aged members). Indeed, pensions expert Ros Altman has noted that the government's own pension vehicle set up for the management of contributions through its auto-enrolment scheme would not be compliant with the charge cap:

> The charge structure of the taxpayer-backed NEST scheme does not properly fit with the aims of a simple charge cap. For a charge cap to work most effectively, customers must be able to easily compare schemes with each other. Two-tier charge models make this difficult. NEST has an initial contribution charge of 1.8% plus a 0.3% AMC annual fee, while NOW: pensions charges an

£18 initial fee, plus 0.3% AMC – these cannot easily be compared with schemes that have a TER [total expense ratio] of 0.5%. The Pensions Policy Institute calculates that older workers in NEST are particularly disadvantaged. Those who are auto-enrolled at age 60 and contribute until their state pension age will pay far more in charges with NEST than with a 0.75% cap. As it is older workers who will retire first under auto-enrolment, it is disappointing that reform of NEST's charges has not been included.[22]

But different products of a similar generic type rarely cost exactly the same; and costs are different in respect of consumers with different sized funds or where members expect to be contributing for a short period of time. Uniform charges where costs are not uniform is a recipe for highly distorted markets with many parts of the population left under-served.

Indeed, the 2013 DWP Charges Survey noted that scheme size was one of the main factors determining charges.[23] However, the DWP argues that members of different size schemes should face the same levels of charges. In other words, the government seeks to make cross subsidies in the pensions market compulsory. This is a policy that seems designed to lead to pension providers withdrawing either explicitly or implicitly (through targeted marketing) from those parts of the market that currently serve smaller employers and less-well-off and some older employees. Indeed, the government argued in its own consultation on charge caps that members of smaller schemes would benefit most because members of larger schemes enjoyed lower charges (DWP 2014: 57). If larger schemes enjoy lower charges because they are intrinsically cheaper to manage, imposing charge caps will simply

---

22 http://pensionsandsavings.com/pensions/pension-charge-cap-another-piece-of
-the-jigsaw/ (accessed 10 March 2015).

23 https://www.gov.uk/government/publications/defined-contribution-pen
sion-schemes-landscape-and-charges-survey-2013 (accessed 10 March 2015).

distort the market and could lead to poor-quality provision or no provision at all for some groups.

In fact, the 2013 DWP Charges Survey would suggest that the market behaves in a rational way and produces the result that would be expected in a market with workable competition. According to the survey, the key determinants of the annual management charge were the size of the scheme (bigger schemes had significantly lower charges); the level of commission; the level of contributions; and the age of the scheme (older schemes had higher charges as innovation and competitive pressure have since driven down costs and charges). Why are price caps to be introduced in a market that seems to be functioning well? Furthermore, why are price caps to be structured in a way that will encourage cross subsidies and reduce competition? The answer to this question, once again, is that politicians wish to set charges on pension scheme investment funds in order to seek applause from expressive interests who lack the information and incentives to assess the costs and benefits of the policy.

(d) *Charge caps and 'whack a mole'.* Charges on pension funds can cover the provision of a number of services provided by the pension company. Typically, as noted, costs are much higher when a pension product has just been sold. Traditionally, providers have tried to recoup these 'set-up' costs through a level annual charge, where the charge is higher than their costs in later years and lower than their costs in earlier years. If such an annual charge is capped at an uneconomic level, providers might well try to charge employers who set up pension schemes separately for the initial services they provide (for example, set-up costs, costs of advice, initial administration, and so on). Once again, this problem was noted by the government (DWP 2014: 45):

> Another theme that emerged in several responses was the risk of more frequent 'employer charges'. Often providers offer

middleware services to employers free of charge, and build the cost of these into the members' charges. Following the introduction of a default fund charge cap, providers may shift responsibility for these costs onto employers.

The document went on to note that the existence of such changes may mean that, once an employer had set up a fund, they might be unwilling to switch providers even if it was in the best interests of members to do so, as employers would have to incur these initial set-up costs again. This could then reduce competition as the DWP itself noted.

Anticipating that a charge cap on pension products might lead to employers being charged directly for particular services, the government indicated that such charges might be banned. The next step could then be to charge employees directly, but it is hardly likely that, if charges levied on employers would not be tolerated by the government, direct charges on employees would be. Thus regulation begets further regulation.

The same – and related – issues arise with regard to the structure of investment funds. If charges are capped, it is less likely that niche investment categories, which are expensive to manage, will be offered to members of pension funds, even if they provide significant benefits. Alternatively, pension providers may offer funds with different structures that hide charges. For example, a fund investing in real estate may incur high charges, but these could be hidden by using a fund which invests in real estate investment companies. Very low charges could be charged by the fund while the real estate investment companies themselves incur high management costs. Such devices to repackage charges could be used in other niche areas of investment management such as international equity investment in emerging markets, infrastructure funds and private equity. Surely they would then attract regulation too.

The government has also indicated that it will ban firms that reward persistent savings behaviour by giving discounts to active members who are still paying contributions. This would seem to be a difficult policy to justify. In terms of its possible impacts, it is worth noting that switching in electricity markets has fallen by 50 per cent since the energy regulator banned selective discounts in 2008.[24] The result of the policy of banning selective discounts in energy markets was that charges rose for the minority but did not fall for the majority, and competition was undermined.

When regulation distorts the market and undermines competition, both consumers and service providers will respond. Politicians will then respond to the attempts to avoid simple regulation by introducing more complex and comprehensive regulation.

Conclusion

Price regulation in financial markets does not have an illustrious history. Proposals for ceilings on charges have recently been developed for large areas of the UK's already heavily regulated consumer finance markets. There are many undesirable consequences of such regulation. For example, the evidence suggests that vulnerable consumers can be driven underground. In the market for pensions, charge caps could impede competition and create price stickiness so that price ceilings simultaneously become floors. Politically regulated charges can be determined by vested interests, rent-seeking groups and politicians seeking the short-term appreciation of voter groups who are (rationally) not well informed about the issues.

There is evidence that these areas of consumer financial markets work well without charge caps. Furthermore, certainly in the case of pensions, other actions could be taken to lower costs by increasing competition. For example, McClymont and Tarrant

---

24 Evidence to House of Commons Energy and Climate Change Select Committee. http://www.publications.parliament.uk/pa/cm201314/cmselect/cmenergy/108/108vw23.htm (accessed 10 March 2015).

(2013) have, along with an industry trade body, the National Association of Pension Funds, proposed that trust-based pension schemes should be able to scale up to achieve economies of scale and develop forms of governance so that members are represented more effectively.[25] Existing and forthcoming government regulation already pushes up the costs of pensions and customers would benefit from liberalisation. For example, the forthcoming EU regulation of insurers, known as Solvency II, could reduce pension annuities by between 5 and 20 per cent, dwarfing any benefits from charge caps, even if caps have the benefits their proponents suggest.

If new regulations in relation to charges were to be introduced, they could take the form of a very simple requirement on employers to explain to employees why their pension provider was significantly more expensive than the National Employment Savings Trust[26] if it were so. This would be a simple measure that would improve information flows and competition. It would also be a stable measure that would not lead to pressure for further regulation. While the authors do not believe that such regulation is necessary, it would certainly be better than alternative proposals.

References

Brennan, G. and Lomasky, L. (1993) *Democracy and Decision: The Pure Theory of Electoral Preference*. Cambridge University Press.

Caplan, B. (2007) *The Myth of the Rational Voter: Why Democracies Choose Bad Policies*. Princeton University Press.

Department for Work and Pensions (2014) Better Workplace Pensions: Further Measures for Savers. Her Majesty's Stationery Office. https://

---

25 It should be noted that the authors of this paper also called for charge caps.

26 This was set up as a government initiative but has ambiguous ownership. It operates according to commercial disciplines with its capital obtained from the private sector.

www.gov.uk/government/consultations/better-workplace-pen
sions-a-consultation-on-charging (accessed 10 March 2015).

Mayer, R. (2012) Loan sharks, interest-rate caps, and deregulation. *Washington and Lee Law Review* 69(2), article 10. http://scholarly commons.law.wlu.edu/wlulr/vol69/iss2/10 (accessed 10 March 2015).

McClymont, G. and Tarrant, A. (2013) *Pensions at Work, that Work – Completing the Unfinished Pensions Revolution*. Fabian Ideas 633. London: The Fabian Society.

Morgan, D. P. and Strain, M. R. (2008) Payday holiday: how households fare after payday credit bans. Federal Reserve Bank of New York Staff Reports 309.

Ofgem (2011) *The Retail Market Review – Findings and Initial Proposals*. London: Ofgem.

Office of Fair Trading (2014) *Defined Contribution Workplace Pension Market Study*. London: OFT.

Policis (2004) *The Effects of Interest Rates Controls in Other Countries*. London: DTI.

Tullock, G. (2006) *The Vote Motive*, Hobart Paperback 33. London: Institute of Economic Affairs.

9 UNIVERSITY PRICE CONTROLS

Steven Schwartz

I believe there's something out there watching over us. Unfortunately, it's the government.

Woody Allen

In 1998, the government set undergraduate university fees at £1,000 per year.[1] If prices increased in line with inflation, the fee today (late 2014) would be £1,537. Instead, the average university charges almost five times this amount (£8,647) (Paton 2013).[2] This stratospheric price rise would constitute a strong argument for government-mandated controls except for one problem – the government did control university fees over the entire 16-year period. And it still does. Without government price ceilings, university fees would probably have soared even higher. Vice-chancellors certainly wanted them to. Even now, they claim that the £9,000 price ceiling is below the market rate (some say it is below their costs).[3] Yet, the same vice-chancellors are preparing to increase their student numbers by 30,000 (Graham 2013). Irrational? Incomprehensible? Perverse? Welcome to the topsy-turvy world of higher education.

---

1   In the UK, responsibility for universities has been devolved to the individual countries. This chapter focuses on public universities in England with a few references to other UK countries, to universities further afield and to for-profit institutions.

2   In 2015, the average fee will rise to £8,830.

3   Andrew Hamilton, Oxford Vice-Chancellor's Oration (2013).

The aim of this chapter is to explain why university price controls have been so ineffective. Along the way, we will take a Willie Wonka tour through the arcane world of higher education. Like Charlie in the chocolate factory, you will be amazed, puzzled and sometimes a little frightened by what you see.

Higher education is a business

Visit a UK university and you are bound to see impressive buildings (both new and ancient). At some point, you may also encounter a decorative crest which looks like a medieval coat of arms. The crest is usually accompanied by a motto, normally in English but sometimes rendered in Latin, Gaelic or Welsh. The formal buildings, crests and mottoes combine to convey a seriousness of purpose, a sense of history and an aura of prestige.

To judge by their mottoes, universities have noble aims (for example, 'truth lies open to all'; 'let us seek higher things'; and 'for the common good'). These are platitudes, of course, but there is truth in them – universities are vital social institutions. They educate the next generation of leaders; their research deepens our understanding of our world; and they promote social mobility by giving people from all walks of life a chance to realise their full intellectual potential.

Their purposes are lofty and worthwhile, but it is important to keep in mind that universities are also businesses. They purchase equipment, consume supplies and employ labour to create products and services, which they sell at a price. Costs constrain the volume and quality of their output, and revenues influence which services and products they provide (Winston 1999). If their income fails to exceed their expenditures, then universities eventually go bankrupt. In short, universities display the characteristics of a normal business.

University income comes from a variety of sources: government subsidies; student fees; philanthropic donations; research contracts; commercial patents; branch campuses in foreign countries; credentialing; spin-out companies; property development; consulting; investment returns; and an array of sub-businesses (catering, conferences, accommodation, souvenir T-shirts). These revenues can add up – Cambridge University's yearly income is around £1.4 billion[4] – yet few universities make profits. This is not bad management; it is entirely deliberate. Except for a small number of proprietary institutions, universities – both public and private – are not-for-profit enterprises. This status not only gives them generous tax advantages, but it also makes universities attractive to philanthropists (who is going to donate money to BP, HSBC or Apple?). Non-profit status is also good for public relations. Students, parents and even business leaders seem to trust not-for-profit institutions more than they trust profit-making ones (Rose-Ackerman 1996).

Although they are not-for-profit businesses, successful universities make money. Cambridge University finished the 2012 financial year with a 'surplus' of more than £70 million.[5] Unlike profit-making businesses, universities do not distribute their surpluses to shareholders. Instead, they use them to improve teaching, conduct research, construct new facilities, purchase equipment and award bursaries to needy students. Universities also use their surpluses to provide staff with higher salaries, managers with better perks and students with more lavish facilities. Just because an institution is not-for-profit does not mean that no one benefits.

University price controls are ubiquitous

The problems caused by price controls have been known since biblical times (Schuettinger and Butler 1979). If a price floor is

---

4   University of Cambridge (2013) Reports and financial statements for the year ended 31 July.

5   University of Cambridge, op. cit.

set too high, there will be surpluses. If a price ceiling is set too low, there will be shortages. This is the conventional wisdom. Unfortunately, when it comes to universities, the conventional wisdom is widely ignored. In England, the government imposes a price ceiling of £9,000 per year on the fees paid by home and EU undergraduates in public universities. Most universities charge the full £9,000 and, as already noted, the average charge is only a little lower (£8,647).[6] Too low, say universities, yet there is no shortage of places.

Price controls are not unique to England. They apply to public university fees in Australia, Canada, the US, most European and South American countries and most Asian countries as well.[7] Some countries, including the UK, also apply price controls to the fees charged by private higher education providers (Estrada 2014).[8] In the US, President Obama has proposed tying federal government grants and subsidies to the tuition fees charged by private universities (the higher the fee, the lower the subsidy). This is an indirect way of controlling their prices.[9]

Why do governments seek to control university tuition fees? There are two answers to this question: the first is political and the second is economic. Let us start with the politics.

The politics of price controls

Thirty years ago, higher education was the preserve of a small elite (Bolton 2012). Today it is perceived as a necessity for anyone

---

6   The maximum fee for part-time students is £6,750.

7   In the US and Canada, state and provincial governments rather than the central government set university tuition prices. In England and Australia, tuition fees are controlled by the central government.

8   In England, students seeking access to government loans, who are studying with private higher education providers, cannot be charged more than £6,000 per year.

9   *The White House Fact Sheet on the President's Plan to Make College More Affordable: A Better Bargain for the Middle Class* (2013). Washington, DC: The White House.

seeking a well-paid career. With so many people affected, any fee increase instantly becomes a political hot potato. President Obama summarised the politics of university prices in a recent speech at the University of Buffalo.[10] Noting that American university tuition fees tripled over the last 30 years while family incomes rose only 16 per cent, he went on to say:

> At a time when a higher education has never been more important or more expensive, too many students are facing a choice that they should never have to make: Either they say no to college and pay the price for not getting a degree – and that's a price that lasts a lifetime – or you do what it takes to go to college, but then you run the risk that you won't be able to pay it off because you've got so much debt.[11]

Soaring tuition fees, increasing debt and historically high levels of unemployment among graduates have combined to make voters unhappy – and no politician likes to do that. When the English university fee ceiling jumped from £3,290 to £9,000, the backlash delivered a blow to the Liberal Democrats from which they never recovered.[12] This is a salutary lesson for any politician. Governments set price ceilings to show voters that they 'feel their pain'.

Despite the ferocious reaction that always accompanies fee increases, students do not seem to be particularly deterred by higher prices. A year after the £9,000 fee ceiling was introduced, university applications dropped a little but the numbers quickly bounced back to near record levels (Grove 2014; Paton 2014). Students seem to be relatively insensitive to university

---

10 The White House Blog, 22 August 2013. President Obama explains his plan to combat rising college costs.

11 Ibid.

12 Kingston students ditch Lib-Dems after tuition fee hike. (2012). River. 25 October.

price increases. There are three reasons for their apparent insouciance.

Students are not required to pay their fees up front.[13] The government lends students the money to pay their fees; these loans are repaid years later once graduates are working. Postponing payment appears to mute price signals (Chapman et al. 2014). The second reason that students seem insensitive to price rises is their tendency to view a higher tuition fee as a proxy for a higher quality education. That is, for many students, higher education is a 'Veblen good' for which demand *increases* in line with price (Veblen 1957; Fisher 1993). The third reason is the lack of cheaper alternatives. When they were given the opportunity to increase tuition fees, practically all universities raised their fees to the maximum (£9,000). Students who preferred to pay less had nowhere to go.

As discussed in the next section, the 'income-contingent' loan system has many advantages, but it also has the potential to increase costs. Avoiding such an increase in costs was the second reason that government set price ceilings in the UK – and why governments do so more generally.

Containing the effects of moral hazard

Universities are the 'marshaling yards for life's gravy train' (Ellis 1995). Graduates get the best jobs and make the highest salaries. Because of the personal benefits they receive, it is fair that students fund at least part of the cost of their education. This presents a problem for bright students from low-income backgrounds. If they wish to study, they must borrow the money. But banks are reluctant to make student loans. As Bruce Chapman

---

13 Australian experience shows that students do not simply ignore university prices. When they were given a discount for paying their fees up front (not taking out a loan) many Australians chose to save the money and forgo the debt. This is not an option in the British system.

points out, slavery has long been abolished, so there is no collateral for banks to sell should a graduate default (Chapman 2011: 86). Banks will only make loans to students if some creditworthy entity (usually the government) provides them with a guarantee. This is what happens in the US. As an alternative, the government could borrow on its own credit and use the money to make student loans: this is the English system. However, government loans are not just for students from low-income backgrounds; all students are eligible. Graduates repay their loans once their income reaches an earnings threshold (currently £21,000).

These 'income-contingent' loans are arguably an efficient, fair and attractive solution to the reluctance of banks to invest in human capital (Chapman 2005). Unlike traditional mortgage-style loans, it is impossible to default on an income-contingent loan because repayments are matched to a graduate's income. Those who lose their jobs, take time off to have children or never reach the earnings threshold have no obligation to make payments. In addition, the government writes off all unpaid student loans after 30 years.

Income-contingent loans make access to higher education dependent on whether students can benefit rather than whether they have the upfront capital. However, they also have a downside. If graduates never earn enough money to repay their fees, taxpayers absorb the loss. In tough economic times, these losses can mount up. Current estimates suggest that 45 per cent of English student loans will be written off as uncollectable, and there are £10 billion in student loans made every year (Bolton 2014).

Although they serve a worthy social purpose, income-contingent loans also provide many opportunities for moral hazard (encouragement to take risks while somebody else bears the consequences) (Chapman 2005). For example, because universities receive their fees up front and are not responsible for collecting loan repayments, they may be tempted to admit academically marginal students. After all, it is not the universities but the taxpayers that will have to bear the losses. Universities would be much more careful about whom they admit and which courses they offer if they were making student loans than if the government guarantees loans.

Moral hazard also applies to students. The loan system encourages students to borrow more than they would if loan repayments were not income-contingent. This is because the government is taking most of the risk. If graduates benefit from their education and reach the income threshold, they repay their loans. If they never reach the income threshold, they are not required to make repayments, and the government absorbs the loss. Imagine offering loans to stock market speculators on similar terms. If their investments are successful, they repay their loan and keep the profit; if their investments collapse, the taxpayer makes good their losses. Who wouldn't accept such a deal?

The income-contingent loan system insulates universities and students from losses while the government (on behalf of the taxpayer) bears most of the risk. No wonder governments feel they need to mandate price ceilings.

The story so far

English universities are businesses (albeit mostly not-for-profit) whose prices are mandated by the government for political reasons and as a way of mitigating the moral hazard that arises from the income-contingent loan scheme. Unfortunately, the government's efforts to control prices have so far been largely futile. Despite 16 years of government-mandated tuition fee control, university fees managed to increase much faster than the rate of inflation. Governments continually increased the price 'ceiling' while, at the same time, they reduced direct subsidies to universities. They hoped to lower the cost to the taxpayer by placing more of the costs on students. Unfortunately, this has not worked because taxpayers absorb unpaid loans. The government has merely traded direct subsidies to universities for subsidies to students saving little money in the process.

Under any funding regime, savings are notoriously hard to make because universities suffer from the economic malaise known as the cost disease (Bowen 2012).

The cost disease in universities

Although advanced technology can be found all around universities, it has had little effect on university work. Stuck in the 19th century, higher education is a pre-industrial industry in which academics handcraft bespoke courses, deliver them to students and assess their learning (Schejbal 2012). Lectures and tutorials remain ubiquitous. This is why every university has a multitude of lecture theatres, and considerable administrative effort goes into deciding who gets to use each one, and when. Except for Friday afternoons, lecture theatres are heavily booked and lecturers are always demanding that more be built.

Over the years, the acoustics of lecture theatres has improved, digital projectors have been installed, and air conditioning has made them more comfortable but – as far as teaching is concerned – productivity gains have come mainly from increasing class sizes. As for its core teaching method, it still takes one hour to deliver a one-hour lecture just as it did in the Middle Ages, when our oldest universities were founded.

Over the centuries, productivity has surged in most parts of the economy, driving salaries ever higher. To attract academics from alternative occupations, their wages rose as well. There is still a considerable range of academic salaries, especially in the US, where 'adjuncts' and 'non-tenure-track' academics earn only one-quarter of the salary of a tenured professor (Curtis and Thornton 2014). However, all academic salaries – even the low ones – rise in proportion to salaries in the general economy. Because salaries generally rise faster than inflation, the cost of running a university also rises faster than inflation. The bottom line is that universities require more money in real terms each year to do exactly the same thing they did the year before.

This phenomenon is a version of Baumol's 'cost disease,' named after the economist who first wrote about it (Baumol and Bowen 1966). It applies to the performing arts (it takes the same number of musicians the same amount of time to play Beethoven's fifth symphony today as it did in 1808 when it was first performed). It also applies to barbers, tailors and other labour-intensive industries including higher education.

Ever-increasing costs drive universities to find new sources of income – by enrolling more non-EU foreign students (who are happy to pay more than the price ceiling), from investments, licences, patents and donations. If the income from these sources is still not sufficient to support all the university's activities, vice-chancellors pressure the government to raise the price ceiling. Most governments eventually agree.

To complicate matters further, prices are not the only aspect of university finance controlled by the government. Governments of all political persuasions have tinkered with every aspect of higher education, burying universities under dense sedimentary layers of conflicting rules and regulations. The government not only controls prices, it also controls the output of each individual university.

It does this through a complicated quota system, which limits the number of students that universities may admit. The quota does not apply to all students, only to 'home' (British) and EU undergraduates whose A-level marks are lower than one A and two Bs. (In 2013, the quota only applied to students whose marks were lower than two As and one B.) There is no limit to the number of students with one A and two Bs that a university may admit. The government has announced that it will add 30,000 extra students to the undergraduate home and EU quota for the 2014–15 academic year, and quotas will be abolished altogether in 2015–16 (Graham 2013).

When governments do not interfere, university fees reflect market forces

Undergraduate students who come from countries outside the EU are not subject to a quota or a price ceiling. Universities can enrol as many such students as they wish, and charge them whatever they like. Under these unconstrained conditions, all universities charge students from non-EU countries more than the £9,000 maximum that applies to home and EU students. Australian universities behave similarly – they charge international students higher fees than they charge domestic students whose fees are subject to price ceilings (Norton 2013a). It seems safe to conclude that the £9,000 ceiling is lower than the market-clearing rate.

Also, as we would expect in an unfettered market, different universities charge different prices for their courses. At University College London, for example, fees range from £15,200 for arts to £29,000 for medicine. Liverpool University's non-EU student fee starts at £12,000 for arts courses. The University of Greenwich charges non-EU students a minimum of £10,359 while the University of Bedfordshire's international student fees start at £9,750 only a little more than the price ceiling for home students. The pattern seems clear. When higher education prices and places are unregulated, tuition fees are determined by the demand for the subject (which is why arts degrees are usually the least expensive) and the perceived quality of the institution. In short, without government interference, university prices obey market forces.[14]

Before we conclude that lifting quotas would lead to home and EU students paying prices similar to those paid by non-EU students, we should note one complication. International students pay their fees up front, which means that the amount they can pay is constrained by their budgets. Because home students have access to an income-contingent loan, they do not feel quite

14 Unregulated fees for postgraduates in Australia show a similar pattern.

the same budget pressure. This is one of the reasons why students were undeterred when prices increased to £9,000.

When the Australian government announced that price ceilings would be lifted, the University of Western Australia immediately announced that its tuition fees would double. English universities would no doubt behave similarly. They know from previous experience that most students will not be put off by the higher price tag. If they never earn enough to repay their loans, the taxpayer will absorb the loss. With no price ceiling, these losses could be huge.

Have price controls created a shortage of student places?

Assessing the effect of price ceilings on supply is complicated because it is difficult to determine if any shortage of student places is the result of price controls or quotas, or both.

At present, the best data we have to tease apart the effects of quotas from the effects of price controls comes from Australia. The Australian government began to ease enrolment caps in 2008, but retained price controls (Norton 2013b). Despite a price ceiling that was well below the 'market' price paid by international students, university enrolments grew by 13 per cent and some institutions increased their intake by 20 per cent or more (Norton 2013b). The same phenomenon occurred in England. Universities enthusiastically increased their undergraduate admissions by 30,000 in 2014–15, even though price ceilings remain below the non-EU student price.

But why should lifting quotas result in an increase in student admissions when the price ceiling is set below the market price and may even be lower than the university's costs (Grove 2014; Hamilton, op. cit.)? To understand this apparently irrational behaviour, we must enquire more deeply into what motivates universities.

Universities are motivated by prestige

As we have already noted, university buildings, crests and mottoes are designed to confer prestige. Indeed, the competition for prestige permeates the whole institution. Universities compete at different levels – the elite compete with one another while lower-ranked universities compete among themselves. But, whatever their level, all universities compete. Their common aim is to 'pursue excellence' by continually improving their services, research and facilities (Clotfelter 1996). Because it is notoriously difficult to measure excellence in any absolute way, universities are forced to rely on relative excellence – an institution's standing in relation to others. An entire industry has evolved just for this purpose. It involves the production of university rankings or 'league tables'.

Higher education leaders have numerous complaints about league tables. Nevertheless, all vice-chancellors prefer to see their universities rise up the rankings – and use their positions in publicity. The result is that universities around the world are engaged in a 'perpetual arms race' for prestige (Stocum 2013). Despite huge differences in resources, size and age, all universities are busily trying to 'get to the next level' (Toma 2008).

Getting to the next level requires attracting the best students and the most illustrious staff. Universities want the best students because, unlike the customers of a normal business, students bring more than just money to the transaction (Winston 1999). They also help the university to achieve its educational goals. Students do not learn only from academics, they also learn from one another. By working together on academic projects, participating in clubs and sporting teams and by studying together for examinations, students help one another to learn about leadership, teamwork, tolerance and how to communicate across cultural boundaries. By admitting high-quality students, who are likely to excel in their careers after leaving university, universities also provide their graduates with a valuable network of influential contacts.

Not surprisingly, elite universities are the first choice of high-achieving students. Because they receive many applications, leading universities can be very choosy about which applicants they admit. Under the quota system, good students who miss out on their first-choice university are forced to accept an offer from their second-, third- or even fourth-choice institution. The result is that every university, no matter how unpopular or low quality, exercises some level of selectivity.

This has started to change with the lifting of the quotas on students with high A-level grades. Not surprisingly, most of these high-achieving students wind up in the elite universities. Elite universities are willing to expand their intake of top students because this increases their prestige.[15] All universities charge fees at or near the maximum because no institution wishes to appear cheap or inferior because, as already mentioned, a university's fees are often taken to reflect its quality.

The expansion of elite universities leaves fewer high-performing students for lower-ranked institutions. When quotas disappear entirely in 2015–16, the process of differentiation will accelerate. Elite institutions will take an even higher proportion of the high-performing students, forcing modestly ranked universities to be less selective and lower their entry standards. This is precisely what has happened in Australia since undergraduate quotas were eased (Norton 2013b).

High-performing academics – those with scholarly reputations – also contribute to institutional prestige. This is why universities pay well-known academics higher than average salaries and assign them smaller than average teaching loads. Successful

---

15 Expansion is not an option for Oxford and Cambridge, whose intakes are constrained by the availability of college places. Elite universities may focus entirely on top students while shrinking their numbers of other students. This will enhance their exclusivity and allow them to charge higher prices.

researchers also have preferential access to specialised equipment, university-paid research assistants, paid sabbaticals and, in some cases, jobs for their partners.

Because a university's reputation, particularly its standing in international league tables, is determined by its scholarly output, prestigious universities aspire to increase the quality and quantity of their research.[16] Except for a few research powerhouses, most universities are unable to fund their research from grants, donations and contracts alone. These institutions are forced to divert some of their student fee income to supporting research.

When vice-chancellors claim that the £9,000 price ceiling is below their costs, they do not mean that it costs more than £9,000 per year to teach a student in commerce or accounting or psychology or other popular subjects. They are referring to the cost of teaching these subjects plus the subsidy that goes to support academic research. There is no limit to the size of this subsidy – research opportunities are endless, and there is no ceiling on excellence. This is why universities, engaged in an arms race for prestige, spend so much on research. It is the best way to move up the league tables.

Putting it all together: the effects of price controls on universities

Universities are highly regulated, largely not-for-profit, businesses. They are subject to politically motivated price ceilings, which are also intended to limit the opportunities for moral hazard that arise from the income-contingent loan system. However, a combination of the cost disease, the arms race for prestige and

---

16 As universities are 'schools', you might expect them to be judged on their teaching and learning. However, the main international league tables, such as the one produced by the *Times Higher* or the World Ranking of Universities, rely most heavily on measures of research performance.

the perception that a university's quality is reflected in its fees combine to render price controls largely futile.

What seems irrational behaviour on the part of universities – expanding student numbers at a price vice-chancellors claim is below costs – turns out not to be so mysterious after all. The 'costs' to which they refer include research subsidies. Any price ceiling for university fees will always be below 'costs' because research expenditures have no limit.

In reality, the marginal cost of an additional student in most subjects is low; it is not hard to squeeze another undergraduate into a lecture theatre. Some elite universities are happy to expand the enrolments of high-performing students because these students bring greater prestige. Lower-ranked institutions are also happy to expand enrolments. Their students may have less stellar A-level marks than those attracted to the elite universities, but they bring funds that can be used to fuel the battle for prestige.

History has shown that university price controls have not kept prices from rising. Eliminating price ceilings and quotas for home and EU students would produce market-related price and quality differentiation, just as it has for non-EU students. Recognising this, the Australian government announced in May 2014 that it would seek parliamentary approval to lift all price controls on domestic student fees while making income-contingent loans available to any home student admitted by a university (as noted above, quotas had already been lifted).

With no quotas and no price ceilings, Australian universities will be able to enrol as many domestic students as they wish and charge whatever price they can get away with. Because higher education is a Veblen good and the government provides loans to all students, elite universities will have the opportunity to benefit at taxpayers' expense. Modestly ranked universities, on the other hand, may succumb to moral hazard and admit unprepared students whose fees they get to keep even if graduates never make enough money to repay their loans.

To prevent price gouging and unrestrained admissions, universities must be made to bear at least some of the risk of unpaid loans. They could, for example, be required to repay a proportion of the unpaid loans of their graduates.

To make students more price-sensitive, income-contingent loans should not be written off after 30 years and attempts should be made to recover them from deceased estates. Serious attempts should also be made to recover debts from students who leave the country – if not while they are abroad than when they return home. Passport checks should be able to achieve this.

As this chapter is being written, a hostile Australian parliament is preparing to reject the lifting of university price controls (at least for now). Because the Australian government did not propose the parallel changes to the loan system suggested above, it may end up thankful that it did not get what it wished for.

References

Baumol, W. and Bowen, W. (1966) *Performing Arts, the Economic Dilemma: A Study of Problems Common to Theater, Opera, Music, and Dance*. New York: Twentieth Century Fund.

Bolton, P. (2012) *Education: Historical Statistics*. London: House of Commons.

Bolton, A. (2014) *Student Loan Statistics*. London: House of Commons Library.

Bowen, W. G. (2012) *The 'Cost Disease' in Higher Education: Is Technology the Answer? The Tanner Lectures*. Palo Alto, CA: Stanford University.

Chapman, B. (2005) Income contingent loans for higher education: international reform. Centre for Economic Policy Research Discussion Paper 491, The Australian National University, Canberra.

Chapman, B. (2011) The Australian university student financing system: the rationale for and experience with loans. In *Financing Higher Education and Economic Development in East Asia* (ed. S. Armstrong and B. Chapman). Canberra: ANU Press.

Chapman, B., Higgins, T. and Stiglitz, J. E. (eds) (2014) *Income Contingent Loans: Theory, Practice and Prospects*. Basingstoke, UK: Palgrave Macmillan.

Clotfelter, C. T. (1996) *Buying the Best: Cost Escalation in Elite Private Education*. Princeton University Press.

Curtis, J. W. and Thornton, S. (2014) *The Annual Report on the Economic Status of the Profession*. Washington, DC: American Association of University Professors.

Ellis, W. (1995) *The Oxbridge Conspiracy*. London: Penguin.

Estrada, M. (2014) Price controls in, profits out, for Ecuador's private universities. *PanAm Post*, 23 May.

Fisher, R. D. (1993) Higher education as a Veblen good: the influence of social preferences on the demand for admission to college. Doctoral Thesis, University of Chicago.

Graham, G. (2013) Autumn Statement 2013: cap on student recruitment lifted for all universities. *The Telegraph*, 5 December.

Grove, J. (2014). University applicant numbers hit near record levels. *Times Higher Education*, 31 January.

Norton, A. (2013a) *Mapping Higher Education*. Melbourne: Grattan Institute.

Norton, A. (2013b) *Keep the Caps Off! Student Access and Choice in Higher Education*. Melbourne: Grattan Institute.

Paton, G. (2013) Cost of a degree 'to rise to £26,000' after tuition fee hike. *The Telegraph*, 11 July. https://unistats.direct.gov.uk (accessed 10 March 2015).

Paton, G. (2014). Why straight-As aren't good enough for Oxbridge. *The Telegraph*, 20 July.

Rose-Ackerman, S. (1996) Altruism, nonprofits and economic theory. *Journal of Economic Literature* 34: 701–28.

Schejbal, D. (2012) In search of a new paradigm for higher education. *Innovative Higher Education* 37: 5.

Schuettinger, R. L. and Butler, E. F. (1979) *Forty Centuries of Wage and Price Controls: How Not to Fight Inflation*. Washington, DC: The Heritage Foundation.

Stocum, D. L. (2013) *Killing Public Higher Education*. Oxford: Academic Press.

Toma, J. D. (2008) Positioning for prestige in American higher education: case studies of strategies at four public institutions toward 'getting to the next level'. Paper presented at the 2008 Conference Association for the Study of Higher Education, Jacksonville, FL, November.

Veblen, T. (1957) *The Higher Learning in America: A Memorandum on the Conduct of Universities by Businessmen*. New York: Sagamore Press.

Winston, G. C. (1999) Subsidies, hierarchy and peers: the awkward economics of higher education. *Journal of Economic Perspectives* 13(1): 1–16.

10 MINIMUM UNIT PRICING

Christopher Snowdon

What is minimum pricing?

Minimum unit pricing (MUP) creates a floor price below which retailers cannot sell a unit of alcohol. A unit of alcohol is 10 ml of pure ethanol and there are two to three units in a typical pint of beer. At the 50p rate advocated by public health campaigners, it would be illegal to sell a can of standard strength lager below £1.00, a bottle of wine below £5.25 and a bottle of spirits below £14.00.[1]

Supporters of the policy say that minimum pricing is preferable to tax rises because it directly targets the cheapest alcohol that tends to be bought by the heaviest drinkers. They argue that tax rises are frequently not passed on to the customer because the drinks industry absorbs the costs (although Leicester (2011: 22) finds evidence that alcohol taxes, on average, are passed on with interest) and they say that that minimum pricing targets problem drinkers while having little impact on 'responsible drinkers'.

Since Britain has some of the highest rates of alcohol duty in the world, MUP is seen as a way of tackling excessive drinking without raising the price of premium beverages or penalising those who drink in pubs and restaurants. By contrast, opponents of the policy argue that cheap alcohol is disproportionately

---

1 Based on 5 per cent, 14 per cent and 40 per cent alcohol by volume respectively.

purchased by people on low incomes and that MUP is therefore discriminatory and regressive.

Minimum unit pricing of alcohol is the subject of fierce political debate in the UK. The Scottish government has passed legislation to implement such a policy, though implementation is currently stalled pending a reference to the European Court of Justice. The UK government has considered and rejected the policy, though it is still very firmly in the ministerial in-tray of potential policy options and could easily be revived.

Theoretical evidence

The system of minimum pricing proposed in Britain does not currently exist anywhere in the world, although a somewhat similar scheme operates in the state alcohol monopolies of some Canadian provinces. In the absence of real world evidence, a predictive model created by researchers at Sheffield University has assumed a remarkable degree of influence in the debate about whether minimum pricing 'works'.

The Sheffield Alcohol Pricing Model (SAPM) first estimated the consequences of minimum pricing in 2008 and has produced several updated projections for England and Scotland in the years since. Its combined output now runs to many hundreds of pages and is the source of some highly specific claims, including the prediction that minimum pricing in Scotland will save 63 lives in its first year, while in England it will 'save 3,393 lives and reduce hospital admissions by 97,900' (after ten years) (Rae 2012).

The Sheffield model is fed with price elasticity estimates, crime figures and health data in an effort to predict the effect of minimum pricing on alcohol consumption, health outcomes, crime, productivity and consumer spending. The first version of the model predicted that a 40p minimum unit price would reduce alcohol consumption by 2.6 per cent at a cost of £21.52 per drinker per annum, leading to 1,381 fewer alcohol-related deaths per annum after a decade (Brennan et al. 2008: 112, 114). The most recent version projects that a 45p minimum price will reduce consumption by 1.6 per cent at a cost of £2.12 per drinker, reducing deaths by 860 per annum after a decade.

Minimum pricing is portrayed as a more targeted intervention than alcohol tax hikes because it only raises the price of the cheaper drinks that are disproportionately purchased by 'hazardous' and 'harmful' drinkers (the two categories are separate in the SAPM; the latter being the heaviest drinkers). The success of the policy therefore depends on the extent to which the heaviest consumers reduce their alcohol intake. In economic terms, this depends on their elasticity of demand, but price elasticities are neither derived from, nor designed for, situations in which the price of the cheapest products alter while the rest of the category remains the same. The lack of real world evidence necessarily requires untested assumptions about how own-price and cross-price elasticities[2] would interact in this unusual scenario. Some degree of uncertainty is therefore inevitable, but there are several questionable assumptions in the SAPM that lead to a probable exaggeration of the benefits and an underestimation of the costs.

Firstly, the price elasticities in the model are high and have become higher since the first edition was published. In the first SAPM, the own-price elasticity of beer was −0.53, implying that a 10 per cent price rise would reduce consumption by 5.3 per cent, but by 2014 this had nearly doubled to −0.98, meaning that the same price rise would reduce consumption by nearly 10 per cent. Wine also became more elastic, although spirits became dramatically less elastic, falling from −0.62 to just −0.08. The price

---

2   The own-price elasticity measures how much the demand for a product changes when its price changes. The cross-price elasticity measures how much the demand for a product changes when the price of a rival product changes (e.g. butter and margarine) or the price of a complementary product changes (e.g. tonic water and gin).

elasticity of cider was left out of earlier versions of the SAPM but when it was later introduced it was assumed to have a very elastic demand of –1.27. The figures for beer and cider, in particular, are at the higher end of estimates found in the economic literature. The meta-analyses of Fogarty (2006), Gallet (2007), Wagenaar et al. (2009) and Nelson (2014) all report own-price elasticities for beer lower than –0.5, for example. The assumption that drinkers are highly price sensitive means that price rises in the SAPM have a more profound effect on alcohol consumption – and, therefore, on health – than would otherwise be expected.

Secondly, the Sheffield researchers assume that heavy and harmful drinkers are more price sensitive than moderate drinkers. This, again, represents a divergence from the mainstream economic literature. Most empirical work confirms the common sense view that heavy consumers have a relatively inelastic demand for alcohol and that the most dependent drinkers may have 'perfectly price inelastic demands' (Manning et al. 1995). The same is true of the other group that minimum pricing intends to target – teenagers – who are 'least responsive to price' (Gallet 2007: 133). Moderate consumers, by contrast, are more price sensitive (Wagenaar et al. 2009). The Sheffield researchers are aware of this literature but ultimately choose to ignore it, instead basing their model on the reverse hypothesis that heavy drinkers are more price sensitive than average (Brennan et al. 2008: 51).

Thirdly, the SAPM makes no distinction between high and low strength beverages when estimating the elasticity of demand. This is critically important in the case of cider and beer. High strength white cider and Somerset scrumpy are, to all intents and purposes, different products. Similarly, Special Brew and real ale, while both being classed as beer, are qualitatively different in terms of strength, use and customer demographic. The high strength variants of beer and cider are heavily associated with alcoholics, who, by definition, have an inelastic demand. However, in the absence of accurate price elasticities for high strength varieties, the SAPM relies on estimates based on average strength products. It assumes that the price elasticity of super strength lager is identical to that of a craft ale and vice versa.

The perverse consequences of constructing the model in this way can be illustrated by the fact that a heavy and dependent drinker who consumes high strength cider is considered by the SAPM to be more likely than any other drinker to reduce their consumption as a result of minimum pricing. This runs counter to a significant body of evidence showing that such drinkers have an elasticity of demand for alcohol that is 'not significantly different from zero' (Purshouse et al. 2009: 76).

The Sheffield model is an extremely thorough piece of work in many respects. It includes a vast number of figures on all sorts of different variables, often calculated to several decimal places, but a model is only as good as the assumptions that are fed into it and many of the assumptions in the SAPM are highly questionable. The mathematical precision of the Sheffield estimates, along with their confident presentation to the media over several years, has given the impression that they are only a hair's breadth from being hard evidence. In fact, they are flawed and highly speculative.

Real world evidence

A study from British Columbia, where a form of minimum pricing has been in place for many years, purported to show that the policy successfully reduces the number of alcohol-related deaths (Zhao et al. 2013). It claimed that a 10 per cent hike in the minimum price had led to a sensational 32 per cent decline in alcohol-related mortality. Although touted as real world evidence, this was also an extrapolation based on a computer model and its headline finding is not supported by data from the Canadian government.

The minimum price for beer and spirits increased in British Columbia several times in the first decade of this century[3] and the study's authors claimed that there was a large drop in wholly alcohol-attributable deaths in 2006–7 (Stockwell 2013). However, official statistics show that the alcohol mortality rate rose from 26 per 100,000 persons to 28 per 100,000 persons between 2002 and 2008. As Figure 12 shows, neither mortality (solid line) nor per capita alcohol consumption (dotted line) fell as a result of the increases in the minimum price. Rates of alcohol-related morbidity also rose (from 375 to 457 per 100,000 persons) (CARBC n.d.).

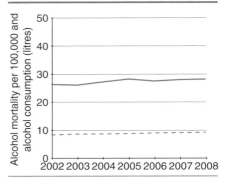

Figure 12 Alcohol-related mortality and alcohol consumption in British Columbia between 2002 and 2008

Between 2002 and 2011, the number of deaths directly attributed to alcohol in British Columbia rose from 315 to 443 per annum, with the largest annual death rates occurring after the minimum price rises of 2006 (see Figure 13) (CARBC 2013: 2). Between 2006 and 2008, when most of the minimum price rises occurred, the number of deaths rose from 383 to a peak of 448 per annum. Moreover, the rate of hospitalisations for both alcohol-related ailments and acute intoxication rose during this decade (Vallance et al. 2012). According to the Centre for Addictions for BC, 'Alcohol consumption in BC has been above the Canadian

3   Minimum price increases between 2002 and 2009:
    Spirits: August 2004 (4.2 per cent), September 2006 (4.9 per cent), January 2008 (3.5 per cent) and April 2009 (4.5 per cent).
    Packaged beer: May 2006 (15.7 per cent) and January 2008 (2 per cent).
    Draft beer: May 2006 (6.3 per cent) and January 2008 (1.8 per cent).
    Other beverages: No change.

Figure 13 Deaths in British Columbia that were directly attributed to alcohol between 2002 and 2011

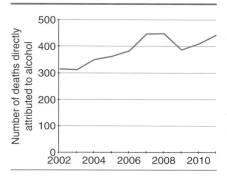

average for the last decade. The rates of hospitalizations in BC for conditions related to alcohol have shown a significant increase since 2002, reflecting an overall increase in alcohol consumption in the province' (Thompson et al. 2013: 2).

In sum, every indicator suggests that alcohol-related health problems worsened somewhat during the period covered by the study. Whatever methods the study's authors used to construct their model, the results bear no resemblance to the recorded facts. There was never a 32 per cent decline in mortality, or anything close to it. Nor, indeed, was there ever a 10 per cent rise in the minimum price; most of the price rises only slightly exceeded the rate of inflation. British Columbia saw trivial changes in real prices, alcohol-related mortality and alcohol consumption. Although the study inspired newspaper reports that stated as fact that 'between 2002 and 2009 deaths described as "wholly alcohol attributable" fell by 32 per cent following a 10 per cent rise in average minimum prices' as well as absurd headlines such as '30p added to cost of pint "can cut alcohol deaths by a third"' (Buckland 2013; Metro 2013), the practical experience of British Columbia tells us very little about the efficacy of minimum pricing.

Financial costs

The Sheffield model uses cross-price elasticities to estimate what substitution effects will be created by minimum pricing within the legal alcohol category. The model projects the extent to which MUP will make people switch from cider to spirits, for example, but it does not account for drinkers switching to illicit alcohol, homemade alcohol or buying alcohol abroad. It does not factor in possible switching from alcohol to illegal drugs. Nor does it tell us about the impact of drinkers cutting their household budget for other products, such as food and heating, in order to maintain their alcohol intake. Unintended consequences such as these are as difficult to predict as the intended consequences on health, but one outcome is almost certain: the nation's expenditure on alcohol will rise under a minimum pricing regime.

The extent to which overall expenditure on alcohol will increase depends on the elasticity of demand and it is likely that the financial burden will fall most heavily on low-income groups, who are more likely to purchase the targeted products. Concerns about MUP being regressive led Gordon Brown to reject minimum pricing when he was prime minister (Hencke and Sparrow 2009) and they have been raised by politicians from all parties ever since. The Australian National Health Prevention Agency twice rejected minimum pricing on the basis that the substitution effects are unknown and the costs are likely to outweigh the benefits (ANPHA 2012, 2013). The agency plausibly concluded that 'total expenditure on alcohol is likely to increase' under MUP (ANPHA 2013: 10). The New Zealand government has come to the same conclusion (Ministry of Justice 2014).

After the Westminster government rejected minimum pricing in 2013, the Sheffield team published a revised model in *The Lancet*, which predicted that the financial impact on low-income and moderate drinkers was less than previously thought (Holmes et al. 2014). The 2010 version of the SAPM estimated that a 45p minimum price would cost drinkers an average of £29.30 per year (Purshouse et al. 2010). The 2014 model, by contrast, claimed that the average cost per drinker would be just £2.12 per year.

The most striking difference between the 2014 model and earlier editions is the projected impact on 'harmful' drinkers. The 2010 SAPM predicted that minimum pricing would cost these consumers, who purchase approximately ten units a day, £137.40 per year. By contrast, the 2014 model claimed that the same 45p minimum price would save them £4.01 per year. Harmful drinkers on low incomes did best of all from the new projections, saving £34.63 per year.

The claim that drinkers will save money as a result of higher prices is counterintuitive and probably wrong. Although it is plausible that higher prices might make drinkers cut down their intake somewhat, it is difficult to imagine them deciding to spend less money on alcohol overall. Even if heavy drinkers do not maintain their alcohol intake by spending more on alcohol – they already spend £2,685 per year according to the SAPM – there is no obvious reason to think that they would actually reduce their alcohol budget. The 2014 model was only able to show savings for some drinkers by relying on exceptionally high price elasticities for beer and cider. The researchers note that 'as off-trade cider accounts for a sufficiently large proportion of the alcohol spend by "low-income male harmful drinkers", the high elasticity of this beverage type leads to these consumers' overall spending on alcohol falling under a 45p MUP' (Meng et al. 2013: 79). As discussed above, it is questionable whether these drinkers are as price sensitive as the SAPM assumes.

Low-income moderate drinkers – the group which politicians express the greatest concern for – went essentially untouched in the 2014 model, paying a mere 4p a year more (Holmes et al. 2014: 3). Moderate drinkers *as a whole* were only projected to spend an extra 78p more per year, in contrast to the £8.70 projected in 2010. This led to headlines such as 'Minimum pricing would have "little impact" on moderate drinkers' (Harrington 2014), but, again, this requires some peculiar assumptions. In the SAPM, a 'moderate drinker' is someone who drinks just 5.5 units per week, the equivalent of two pints of lager. A low-income moderate drinker consumes even less, 4.6 units. This is a fraction of the government's rather austere recommendations for healthy drinking (21 units per week for a man) and more accurately describes a very light drinker rather than a moderate drinker.

Moreover, the 2014 model based its projections on a 45p unit price despite campaigners having long since moved on to a more punitive 50p unit, as endorsed by the Scottish government. The impact of a more realistic 50p price would be more severe on drinkers across the board. In 2011, when the campaign for a 50p minimum price was in full flow, the *average* price paid per unit for beer, cider, spirits and alcopops by 'moderate', 'hazardous' and 'harmful' drinkers alike was less than 50p, with the exception of spirits consumed by moderate drinkers. 60 per cent of beer, 77 per cent of cider, 41 per cent of wine and 60 per cent of spirits were being sold at less than 50p per unit (ibid.: 29). Only wine was bought at an average of more than 50p per unit (Meng et al. 2013: 32).

By focusing on an unrealistically low 45p unit, the 2014 SAPM assumes that only 23 per cent of alcohol is sold below the minimum price and that only one in eight units purchased by moderate drinkers will be made more expensive by the policy. Nevertheless, even a 45p unit would 'directly affect the vast majority of off-licence alcohol consumers' (Leicester 2011: 3) and a 50p unit price would increase the financial cost threefold (Meng et al. 2013: 12).

The claim that minimum pricing will have a negligible impact on moderate consumers therefore relies on a misleading definition of moderate consumption and an unrealistic minimum price. The manner in which minimum pricing ceased to be costly and suddenly became cost-saving for several population subsets in 2014 raises questions about the integrity of the model, while the claim that minimum pricing is not regressive, which is highly questionable at the 45p rate, is quite untenable at the 50p rate.

Welfare costs and benefits

If a drinker buys 10 units of alcohol per week at 46p per unit, he spends £4.60 per week. If the government mandates a 50p minimum unit, he will need to spend £5.00 per week to maintain his intake. Minimum pricing will therefore cost him an extra 40p per week. If, however, the higher prices make him reduce his consumption to 9 units per week, he will spend £4.50 per week and could therefore be said to be saving 10p per week.

This example illustrates how campaigners make claims about minimum pricing benefiting drinkers, but it is fallacious because it does not acknowledge the drinker's loss of consumer surplus. In the example above, the drinker is coerced into losing the benefit he enjoys from his tenth unit of alcohol. He might be saving 10p a week, but his prior purchasing decision reveals that he would rather have the benefit of the extra unit of alcohol. Minimum pricing has relieved him of a consumer surplus and burdened him with a deadweight loss. The drinker cannot win (unless he is wealthy enough to never buy alcohol below 50p per unit). Either he maintains his preferred level of drinking and suffers a financial loss, or he reduces his drinking and suffers a welfare loss.

In our example, the drinker does not even enjoy any health benefits since his pre-intervention drinking habits were well within any reasonable guidelines. In the case of those who consume alcohol at 'hazardous' or 'harmful' levels, minimum pricing advocates assume that drinkers would benefit more from reducing their consumption than from maintaining it, but they cannot possibly know this and, in a free society, it is not their decision to make.

The financial costs of minimum pricing are real, even if campaigners understate them. The welfare costs are simply ignored and, as Jamie Whyte notes, a cost–benefit analysis that does not include the benefits people receive from drinking is no analysis at all (Whyte 2013: 37):

> All consumption has both costs and benefits. Provided consumers are not completely price-inelastic, consumption will decline if prices increase and the costs resulting from consumption will also decrease. We know this in advance of any research.

So, if we choose to ignore the loss of benefits that also comes from reduced consumption, we know in advance the result we will get; we know the policy will appear to produce a benefit. There is no need to invest energy in working out precise price elasticities, the sensitivity of disease and crime to alcohol consumption, and so on. It is all a bluff. The moment researchers decided to ignore the lost benefits of alcohol consumption, their 'result' was assured.

Although the authors of Sheffield model do not attempt to evaluate welfare costs, they do briefly acknowledge their existence, saying: 'If, as argued by some commentators, reductions in consumption itself induced by policy are negative effects, then our results suggest a minimum unit price has a mixture of regressive (consumption) and progressive (health outcomes) effects' (Holmes et al. 2014: 9). This is true, but the regressive effects are not included in the model.

Neither the health benefits nor the pleasure of drinking can be monetised (or, rather, they can only be monetised in a manner that is so arbitrary as to be practically useless). As New Zealand's Ministry of Justice noted in a report that rejected minimum pricing, it is not possible 'to quantify all of the positive externalities alcohol consumption may generate, such as social lubrication effects and the building of social capital' (Ministry of Justice 2014: 9) and so, for all its faults, the SAPM should not be criticised for failing to measure the unmeasurable. It provides estimates of how much more (or less) drinkers will spend under a minimum pricing regime and it estimates what savings, if any, there will be to the health service. It does not - and cannot - tell us whether the welfare costs that result from less drinking exceed the health benefits. Those who campaign for minimum pricing are either unaware of the welfare costs or else feel that they are a price worth paying for the putative health benefits. This is a subjective judgement. It is not, as is often claimed, 'evidence-based policy'.

An estimate of lives saved in a partial equilibrium model can never, on its own, justify the implementation of a given policy. If the sole aim of alcohol policy was to reduce consumption, there would be no limits to how high prices were set. A 50p minimum unit price is no more 'evidence-based' than a 20p minimum price, a 70p minimum price, or no minimum price at all. The Sheffield model includes estimates of what would happen under a whole range of possible interventions, up to and including a 70p minimum price in off-licences and a £1 minimum price in pubs. Unsurprisingly, the model finds that the health benefits rise as the prices rise, but the fact that campaigners and politicians are not (yet) calling for a 70p minimum price or a floor price in pubs demonstrates that they are aware that economic decisions involve trade-offs. The mathematical precision of the SAPM tells us nothing about what *should* be done. It is merely an elaborate exploration of the law of demand.

The windfall fallacy

Evidence from the SAPM suggests that a 50p minimum unit price will result in English drinkers spending in the region of £250 million more on alcohol each year (although this is likely to be an underestimate, for the reasons given above).[4] There is a common belief that this money will be a 'windfall' for retailers and producers. In truth, the policy is likely to make people poorer without making anybody richer.

To understand why, take an example in which there are three brands of beer. For the sake of simplicity, let us say that they each contain one unit of alcohol. The bottom end brand, Budget, retails at 35p. The mid-range brand, Average, retails at 50p. The high end brand, Premium, retails at 60p. Premium costs more

---

4   Based on 35 million drinkers spending an additional £7.20 each, as projected in Meng et al. (2013: 12 and 66).

to produce and is more heavily advertised than Average. Average costs more to produce and is more heavily advertised than Budget. Each beer has a profit margin of 5p.

Under a 50p minimum pricing regime, the price of Budget must rise from 35p to 50p. On the face of it, this suggests that either the manufacturer or the retailer will be able to pocket an extra 15p profit. But who will buy Budget when the superior Average brand is available at the same price? Hardly anybody. The most likely outcome is that sales of Average rise and sales of Budget plummet. This is good news for the makers of Average but there is no net gain for the industry as a whole.

Some might assume that the makers of Average would raise prices to exploit the excess profits that minimum pricing has created, but there are no excess profits in a competitive market and minimum pricing has not removed competition. If the price of Average goes up to 60p, it then has to compete with the superior Premium beer and will lose. Why would consumers pay 60p for a mid-range brand when they could have a top-end drink for the same price? Much better to leave Average as the market leader at the (new) bottom end of the market.

Of course, the makers of Premium could raise their price too, perhaps to 75p, but this would allow a rival company to undercut them with a similar offering. The production and advertising costs of producing a top-end beer would not be affected by minimum pricing and a new rival would be happy to take the same 5p profit margin as Premium previously did.

The same thing would happen if Average decided to lower its production costs in an effort to exploit drinkers who can no longer downgrade to Budget. Lowering production costs would increase Average's profit margin, but a rival would enter the market with a 50p offering of superior quality. Any attempt to create excess profits is thwarted by competition.

What about the retailers? If the government forces up the price of low-end brands by 15p with a mandatory minimum, why shouldn't they slap 15p on all the beers and pocket the difference? The answer, again, is competition. If it was so easy to generate extra profit by raising prices, they would already be doing so. If Tesco raises the price of its beer, people will shop at Asda and vice versa. As in any competitive free market, retailers have an incentive to push prices down, not up. The only way the price of the entire beer category could increase would be if there was collusion between the companies, but neither the producers nor the retailers operate in a cartel and such collusion would be illegal.

The effect of minimum pricing, therefore, will not be to create excess profits for industry, but to wipe out the bottom end of the market. The makers of Budget will either have to withdraw the product from sale (because no one will buy it at 50p) or 'do a Skoda' by spending more money on production and advertising (which would bring the profit margin back to 5p). It would no longer be a budget brand; minimum pricing will make budget brands extinct.

This leaves the question of what happens to the extra £250 million (or so) that drinkers will spend as a result of minimum pricing. Aside from a little more VAT being paid on the sale of more expensive alcohol, this money will be swallowed up by the additional production and marketing costs that are required to make a mid-range product. Drinkers who prefer to purchase budget brands with low production costs will have to buy mid-range brands which have higher production costs. The impact on industry profits is negligible; it is consumers who are denied their first choice preference who lose out.[5]

Minimum pricing and the EU

The European Union says that all trading rules 'enacted by Member States which are capable of hindering, directly or indirectly,

---

5   I'm grateful to Dr Eric Crampton for guiding me towards many of the observations in this section (see Crampton 2012).

actually or potentially, intra-Community trade are to be considered as measures having an effect equivalent to quantitative restrictions' (Case 8/74 Dassonville [1974] ECR 837). Such 'quantitative restrictions' are illegal under Article 34 of the Treaty on the Functioning of the European Union. Case law strongly suggests that minimum pricing falls into this category. In a report prepared for the European Commission in 2009, the RAND corporation noted that 'minimum pricing practices have tended to be seen as trade-distorting by the European courts (as setting an artificial price floor amounts to resale price maintenance, limiting and distorting price competition), and therefore not typically put in place in the EU' (Rabinovich et al. 2009: 90).

Advocates of minimum pricing argue that concerns about public health trump concerns about free trade and that an exception can therefore be made for a policy that aims to reduce alcohol-related ill health, but previous attempts to implement a minimum price for tobacco have fallen foul of EU law and it is unlikely that the European Commission will view alcohol as a more pressing case. The European Court of Justice has never accepted minimum pricing on such grounds in the past, partly because it believes that other options, such as higher taxes, could achieve the same policy objectives without disturbing the internal market.

A communication from the European Commission in November 2012 encouraged member states to steer clear of minimum pricing since it was not compatible with EU law. Directly referring to Scotland's proposed 50p per unit minimum pricing proposal, it said that 'The case-law of the Court of Justice of the European Union ("Court of Justice") is unequivocal to the effect that national legislation imposing minimum pricing in respect of particular products falls within the ambit of the Article 34 TFEU (prohibition on measures having the equivalent effect of impeding imports of products).' While the Commission expressed sympathy for the reasons given by the Scottish government for pushing ahead with the policy, it reminded it that there are 'doubts as to its compatibility with the principle of proportionality' and politely asked it to explore 'the possibility to achieve the objective by other means less restrictive to intra-EU trade' (European Commission 2012).

The European Commission said that minimum pricing could only be legal if it did not raise a barrier to imports and that it could only pass the 'public interest' test if there was no other way of achieving the goal of reducing alcohol consumption. Since it felt that a minimum price of 50p would have an adverse effect on intra-EU imports and that general tax rises on alcohol were a viable alternative, it concluded that minimum pricing 'would be in breach of Article 34 TFEU were it to be adopted without giving due consideration to the above remarks' (ibid.).

The EU has previously ruled against minimum pricing not only for tobacco but also for motor fuel. This case law, combined with the Commission's quite explicit warning to the Scottish government, suggests that any campaign for minimum pricing for alcohol within the EU is likely to hit the legal buffers sooner or later.

Conclusion

Price, advertising and availability are three of the key levers of competition in a free market economy. Since the nineteenth century, temperance campaigners have encouraged the state to control all of these levers in the alcohol market so that the first can be increased and the latter can be restricted. Traditionally, price rises have been achieved by increasing alcohol duty – a policy that is always attractive to cash-strapped governments – but minimum pricing offers a way of controlling prices more directly. Once introduced, it is not hard to imagine the minimum price being raised incrementally on a regular basis at the behest of 'public health' campaigners who will always project greater health benefits from higher prices.

Advocates of minimum pricing are careful to downplay the financial costs of minimum pricing while ignoring the welfare costs altogether. Politicians and the public, however, have shown themselves to be more aware of the trade-offs and are more sceptical of theoretical modelling. A study published in the *European Journal of Public Health* (Katikireddi et al. 2013) interviewed opinion-formers and decision-makers under Chatham House rules and found significant private doubts about the policy. One of the politicians interviewed said that he refused to be 'blinded by some study that's been carried out in an ivory tower somewhere', adding that 'I try to think of what I call sort of logic and human nature and my observation of human nature over a period of time, and I just don't accept that it [minimum unit pricing] will make any great difference to people's behaviour' (ibid.). Similarly, an academic said of the projected impact of MUP that 'to be honest, we don't know. We don't know. We've got models. Sheffield modelling etc, all the taxation stuff but we don't know. And we don't know what's gonna happen to the very heavy, heavily dependent drinkers. We actually don't know and there may be some pluses and minuses' (ibid.).

Scepticism about minimum pricing's ability to tackle heavy and binge drinking seems to be shared by the public, who remain concerned about the impact of higher prices on their own budgets (Lonsdale et al. 2012). In a study based on focus group responses, Banerjee et al. (2010: 55) reported that 'this intervention [minimum pricing] was unpopular. It has connotations of punishment, is thought to be heavy handed without addressing the problem effectively, and would create a financial impact that could not be ignored on the responsible majority (i.e. themselves).'

These concerns are well-founded. The modelling almost certainly over-estimates the health benefits for heavy drinkers and under-estimates the costs to moderate and low-income drinkers. Aside from the government receiving a trivial increase in VAT revenue, nobody will benefit financially from the policy because the extra expenditure will be swallowed up in the costs of producing more expensive alcohol for consumers who would prefer to buy cheaper alcohol.

References

ANPHA (Australian National Preventative Health Agency) (2012) Exploring the public health interest case for a minimum (floor) price for alcohol: Draft report. Canberra: ANPHA.

ANPHA (Australian National Preventative Health Agency) (2013) Exploring the public health interest case for a minimum (floor) price for alcohol: Final report. Canberra: ANPHA.

Banerjee, J., Squires, J. and Parkinson, T. (2010) *Public Perceptions of Alcohol Pricing*. London: Home Office.

Brennan, A., Purshouse, R., Taylor, K. and Rafia, R. (2008) Modelling the potential impact of pricing and promotion policies for alcohol in England: results from the Sheffield Alcohol Policy Model Version 2008(1-1). University of Sheffield.

Buckland, L. (2013) Minimum alcohol pricing could reduce death rate. *The Scotsman*, 7 February.

CARBC (Centre for Addictions Research of BC) (n.d.) Mortality and morbidity age-specific and crude rates (per 100,000) by gender for tobacco, illicit drugs and alcohol, BC, 2002–2008. www.carbc.ca (accessed 10 March 2015).

CARBC (Centre for Addictions Research of BC) (2013) Alcohol-related deaths in British Columbia. University of Victoria.

European Commission (2012) Communication from the Commission – SG (2012) D/52513. 26 November.

Fogarty, J. (2006) The nature of the demand for alcohol: understanding elasticity. *British Food Journal* 108: 316–32.

Gallet, C. (2007) The demand for alcohol: a meta-analysis of elasticities. *Australian Journal of Agricultural and Resource Economics* 51: 121–35.

Harrington, J. (2014) Minimum pricing would have 'little impact' on moderate drinkers. *Morning Advertiser*, 13 May.

Hencke, D. and Sparrow, A. (2009) Gordon Brown rejects call to set minimum prices for alcohol. *The Guardian*, 16 March.

Holmes, J., Meng, Y., Meier, P., Brennan, A., Angus, C., Campbell-Burton, A., Guo, Y., Hill-McManus, D. and Purshouse, R. (2014) Effects of minimum unit pricing for alcohol on different income and socioeconomic groups: a modelling study. *The Lancet*, 10 February.

Katikireddi, S., Bond, L. and Hilton, S. (2013) Perspectives on econometric modelling to inform policy: a UK qualitative case study of minimum unit pricing of alcohol. *European Journal of Public Health* 24(2): 490–95.

Leicester, A. (2011) Alcohol pricing and taxation policies. IFS Briefing Note BN124. London: Institute of Fiscal Studies.

Lonsdale, A., Hardcastle, S. and Hagger, M. (2012) A minimum price per unit of alcohol: A focus group study to investigate public opinion concerning UK government proposals to introduce new price controls to curb alcohol consumption. *BMC Public Health* 12: 1023.

Manning, W. G., Blumberg, L. and Moulton, L. H. (1995) The demand for alcohol: the differential response to price. *Journal of Health Economics* 14(2): 123–48.

Meng, Y., Brennan, A., Holmes, J., Hill-McManus, D., Angus, C., Purshouse, R. and Meier, P. (2013) Modelled income group-specific impacts of alcohol minimum unit pricing in England 2014/15: Policy appraisals using new developments to the Sheffield Alcohol Policy Model (version 2.5). University of Sheffield.

Metro (2013) 30p added to cost of pint 'can cut alcohol deaths by a third'. 7 February.

Ministry of Justice (2014) *The Effectiveness of Alcohol Pricing Policies.* Wellington.

Nelson, J. (2014) Estimating the price elasticity of beer: meta-analysis of data with heterogeneity, dependence, and publication bias. *Health Economics* 33: 180–87.

Purshouse, R., Brennan, A., Latimer, N., Meng, Y. and Rafia, R. (2009) Modelling to assess the effectiveness and cost-effectiveness of public health related strategies and interventions to reduce alcohol attributable harm in England using the Sheffield Alcohol Policy Model version 2.0. University of Sheffield.

Purshouse, R., Meier, P., Brennan, A., Taylor, K. and Rafia, R. (2010) Estimated effect of alcohol pricing policies on health and health economic outcomes in England: an epidemiological model. *The Lancet* 375: 1355–64.

Rabinovich, L., Brutscher, P.-B., de Vries, H., Tiessen, J., Clift, J. and Reding, A. (2009) *The Affordability of Alcoholic Beverages in the European Union*. Cambridge: RAND Europe.

Rae, H. (2012) North East doctors in plea for 50p alcohol unit. *The Journal*, 25 October.

Stockwell, T., Zhao, J., Martin, G., MacDonald, S., Vallance, K., Treno, A., Ponicki, W., Tu, A. and Buxton, J. (2013) Misleading UK alcohol industry criticism of Canadian research on minimum pricing (letter). *Addiction* 108: 1172–75.

Thompson, K., Stockwell, T., Vallance, K., Giesbrecht, N. and Wettlaufer, A. (2013) Reducing alcohol-related harms and costs in British Columbia: a provincial summary report. Centre for Addictions Research of BC, University of Victoria.

Vallance, K., Martin, G., Stockwell, T., Macdonald, S., Chow, C., Ivsins, A., Buxton, J., Tu, A., Sandhu, J., Chu, T. and Fair, B. (2012) Overdose events in British Columbia: trends in substances involved, contexts and responses. Centre for Addictions Research of BC, University of Victoria.

Wagenaar, A., Salois, M. and Komro, K. (2009) Effects of beverage alcohol price and tax levels on drinking: a meta-analysis of 1003 estimates from 112 studies. *Addiction* 104: 179–90.

Whyte, J. (2013) *Quack Policy: Abusing Science in the Cause of Paternalism*. London: Institute of Economic Affairs.

Zhao, J., Stockwell, T., Martin, G., MacDonald, S., Vallance, K., Treno, A., Ponicki, W., Tu, A. and Buxton, J. (2013) The relationship between minimum alcohol prices, outlet densities and alcohol-attributable deaths in British Columbia, 2002–09. *Addiction* 108(6): 1059–69.

ABOUT THE IEA

The Institute is a research and educational charity (No. CC 235 351), limited by guarantee. Its mission is to improve understanding of the fundamental institutions of a free society by analysing and expounding the role of markets in solving economic and social problems.

The IEA achieves its mission by:

- a high-quality publishing programme
- conferences, seminars, lectures and other events
- outreach to school and college students
- brokering media introductions and appearances

The IEA, which was established in 1955 by the late Sir Antony Fisher, is an educational charity, not a political organisation. It is independent of any political party or group and does not carry on activities intended to affect support for any political party or candidate in any election or referendum, or at any other time. It is financed by sales of publications, conference fees and voluntary donations.

In addition to its main series of publications the IEA also publishes a quarterly journal, *Economic Affairs*.

The IEA is aided in its work by a distinguished international Academic Advisory Council and an eminent panel of Honorary Fellows. Together with other academics, they review prospective IEA publications, their comments being passed on anonymously to authors. All IEA papers are therefore subject to the same rigorous independent refereeing process as used by leading academic journals.

IEA publications enjoy widespread classroom use and course adoptions in schools and universities. They are also sold throughout the world and often translated/reprinted.

Since 1974 the IEA has helped to create a worldwide network of 100 similar institutions in over 70 countries. They are all independent but share the IEA's mission.

Views expressed in the IEA's publications are those of the authors, not those of the Institute (which has no corporate view), its Managing Trustees, Academic Advisory Council members or senior staff.

Members of the Institute's Academic Advisory Council, Honorary Fellows, Trustees and Staff are listed on the following page.

The Institute gratefully acknowledges financial support for its publications programme and other work from a generous benefaction by the late Professor Ronald Coase.

Other papers recently published by the IEA include:

Does Britain Need a Financial Regulator? – Statutory Regulation, Private Regulation and Financial Markets
Terry Arthur & Philip Booth
Hobart Paper 169; ISBN 978-0-255-36593-2; £12.50

Hayek's The Constitution of Liberty – An Account of Its Argument
Eugene F. Miller
Occasional Paper 144; ISBN 978-0-255-36637-3; £12.50

Fair Trade Without the Froth – A Dispassionate Economic Analysis of 'Fair Trade'
Sushil Mohan
Hobart Paper 170; ISBN 978-0-255-36645-8; £10.00

A New Understanding of Poverty – Poverty Measurement and Policy Implications
Kristian Niemietz
Research Monograph 65; ISBN 978-0-255-36638-0; £12.50

The Challenge of Immigration – A Radical Solution
Gary S. Becker
Occasional Paper 145; ISBN 978-0-255-36613-7; £7.50

Sharper Axes, Lower Taxes – Big Steps to a Smaller State
Edited by Philip Booth
Hobart Paperback 38; ISBN 978-0-255-36648-9; £12.50

Self-employment, Small Firms and Enterprise
Peter Urwin
Research Monograph 66; ISBN 978-0-255-36610-6; £12.50

Crises of Governments – The Ongoing Global Financial Crisis and Recession
Robert Barro
Occasional Paper 146; ISBN 978-0-255-36657-1; £7.50

… and the Pursuit of Happiness – Wellbeing and the Role of Government
Edited by Philip Booth
Readings 64; ISBN 978-0-255-36656-4; £12.50

Public Choice – A Primer
Eamonn Butler
Occasional Paper 147; ISBN 978-0-255-36650-2; £10.00

The Profit Motive in Education – Continuing the Revolution
Edited by James B. Stanfield
Readings 65; ISBN 978-0-255-36646-5; £12.50

Which Road Ahead – Government or Market?
Oliver Knipping & Richard Wellings
Hobart Paper 171; ISBN 978-0-255-36619-9; £10.00

The Future of the Commons – Beyond Market Failure and Government Regulation
Elinor Ostrom et al.
Occasional Paper 148; ISBN 978-0-255-36653-3; £10.00

Redefining the Poverty Debate – Why a War on Markets Is No Substitute for a War on Poverty
Kristian Niemietz
Research Monograph 67; ISBN 978-0-255-36652-6; £12.50

The Euro – the Beginning, the Middle … and the End?
Edited by Philip Booth
Hobart Paperback 39; ISBN 978-0-255-36680-9; £12.50

The Shadow Economy
Friedrich Schneider & Colin C. Williams
Hobart Paper 172; ISBN 978-0-255-36674-8; £12.50

Quack Policy – Abusing Science in the Cause of Paternalism
Jamie Whyte
Hobart Paper 173; ISBN 978-0-255-36673-1; £10.00

Foundations of a Free Society
Eamonn Butler
Occasional Paper 149; ISBN 978-0-255-36687-8; £12.50

The Government Debt Iceberg
Jagadeesh Gokhale
Research Monograph 68; ISBN 978-0-255-36666-3; £10.00

A U-Turn on the Road to Serfdom
Grover Norquist
Occasional Paper 150; ISBN 978-0-255-36686-1; £10.00

New Private Monies – A Bit-Part Player?
Kevin Dowd
Hobart Paper 174; ISBN 978-0-255-36694-6; £10.00

From Crisis to Confidence – Macroeconomics after the Crash
Roger Koppl
Hobart Paper 175; ISBN 978-0-255-36693-9; £12.50

Advertising in a Free Society
Ralph Harris and Arthur Seldon
With an introduction by Christopher Snowdon
Hobart Paper 176; ISBN 978-0-255-36696-0; £12.50

Selfishness, Greed and Capitalism: Debunking Myths about the Free Market
Christopher Snowdon
Hobart Paper 177; ISBN 978-0-255-36677-9; £12.50

Waging the War of Ideas
John Blundell
Occasional Paper 131; ISBN 978-0-255-36684-7; £12.50

Brexit: Directions for Britain Outside the EU
Ralph Buckle, Tim Hewish, John C. Hulsman, Iain Mansfield & Robert Oulds
Hobart Paperback 178; ISBN 978-0-255-36681-6; £12.50

Other IEA publications

Comprehensive information on other publications and the wider work of the IEA can be found at www.iea.org.uk. To order any publication please see below.

Personal customers

Orders from personal customers should be directed to the IEA:

Clare Rusbridge
IEA
2 Lord North Street
FREEPOST LON10168
London SW1P 3YZ
Tel: 020 7799 8907. Fax: 020 7799 2137
Email: sales@iea.org.uk

Trade customers

All orders from the book trade should be directed to the IEA's distributor:

NBN International (IEA Orders)
Orders Dept.
NBN International
10 Thornbury Road
Plymouth PL6 7PP
Tel: 01752 202301, Fax: 01752 202333
Email: orders@nbninternational.com

IEA subscriptions

The IEA also offers a subscription service to its publications. For a single annual payment (currently £42.00 in the UK), subscribers receive every monograph the IEA publishes. For more information please contact:

Clare Rusbridge
Subscriptions
IEA
2 Lord North Street
FREEPOST LON10168
London SW1P 3YZ
Tel: 020 7799 8907, Fax: 020 7799 2137
Email: crusbridge@iea.org.uk